Latina Filmmakers and Writers: The Notion of Chicanisma Through Films and Novellas

La Mujer Latina Series

By
Jenny Dean

Floricanto Press

Copyright © 2007 by Jennifer Watson Dean
Copyright © 2007 of this edition by Floricanto Press

All rights reserved. Except for brief passages quoted in a review, no part of this book may be reproduced in any form, by photostat, microfilm, xeroraphy, electronic and digital reproduction, or placed in the Internet, or any other means, or incorporated into any information retrieval system, electronic, or mechanical, without written permission of the publisher.

ISBN: 978-0-9796457-1-6

Floricanto Press
650 Castro Street, Suite 120-331
Mountain View, California 94041-2055
www.floricantopress.com

Cover graphics by Lawrence W. Lee

Latina Filmmakers and Writers

Contents

Acknowledgements	7
Chapter 1. Introduction	9
Chapter 2. Chican@: What's in a Word?	14
Chapter 3. Racism in American Society and the Chicana	26
Chapter 4. The Chicana Movement and the Emergence of Chicanisma	36
Chapter 5. Chicana (1979)	53
Chapter 6. Puppet: A Novella (1985)	65
Chapter 7. La Ofrenda (1988)	79
Chapter 8. *Paletitas de Guayaba* (1991)	89
Chapter 9. El Espejo/The Mirror (1991)	99
Chapter 10. Loving Pedro Infante (2001)	106
Chapter 11. Conclusion	114
Appendixes	
The Chicano	120
El Espejo/The Mirror Testimonio	122
Interviews:	
Sylvia Morales	124
Margarita Cota-Cárdenas	143
Susana Blaustein Muñoz	155
Lourdes Portillo	162
Erlinda Gonzáles-Berry	177
Frances Salomé España	192
Denise Chávez	203
References	224
Notes	232
Illustration	16
Index	243

To Rags, to New Mexico and to Chicanas and Chicanos everywhere.

Acknowledgements

First and foremost, I would like to thank my mom and dad for allowing me to pursue my interests in Chicanas without a question as to why, how, when or where. I love and admire you both. Second, I would like to express my sincere gratitude to, and appreciation of, Scott Dean for spending hours driving me back and forth to Zimmerman library and various UNM (University of New Mexico) classes, listening to my excitement about Chican@s and their works, and for also bringing me to New Mexico. Had I not gone to New Mexico, this book would have never happened. That brings me to Dra. María Dolores Gonzáles, my first Chicana profesora, who taught me the history and culture of the Chican@ people and by so doing, taught me to love and respect the Chican@ people. Gracias a Dra. Tey Diana Rebolledo for introducing me to the best literature I have ever read. Thanks to Dr. Gabriel Meléndez for introducing me to Chican@ films. Sincere thanks to all the authors and filmmakers who were willing to do interviews with me about their works: Erlinda Gonzáles-Berry, Denise Chávez, Margarita Cota-Cárdenas, Frances Salomé España, Sylvia Morales, Susana Muñoz and Lourdes Portillo. Thanks to Dra. Tamara Falicov of the University of Kansas for reading over my film chapters, filmmaker interviews and for being an overall mentor of this manuscript. Thank you to Kathy Hartke (Rich, too) for reading the very first draft, for being as critical as possible and for helping point out grammar errors (and I am sure some still exist). Thank you to Liz Baker for also reading a copy, making grammar corrections and providing encouragement. Thank you very much to Lawrence W. Lee for the fantastic image on the front cover—your brilliance and friendship has been tremendously rewarding for me –thank you for your humor, generosity and kindness. Thank you to Pat Henderson for legal advice and the late night giggles. Thank you to Bill Griffiths for riding the emotional rollercoaster of the publishing process with me. I love you. Thank you to Marsh, Spencer and Amy for being my supportive siblings. I love you all. And last, but certainly not least, a thank you to my cat, Rags, for bringing me home and for offering encouragement through purrs. I love you, Freegie.

Chapter 1

Introduction: Chicanisma in Literature and Film

Güera! – pero soy
Chicana! – pero soy
Gringa! – pero soy
Nada! – ay, no, pero SOY!
—Maia Chávez Dean from her poem, "*Gringa/Chicana*"

    As a white woman I have struggled with my credibility in writing this work. I understand that my insight into the plight of the Chicana may not be as accurate as that of a Chicana. After all, it is my belief that unless one is born into a culture, one cannot fully understand that culture. In fact, complete understanding of a culture cannot be achieved unless one experiences it on a daily basis. Therefore, in an effort to make my observations as accurate as possible, I have consulted and verified many of my thoughts and ideas with both Chicana scholars and artists. I have also verified these thoughts and concepts with various scholarly works by Chicanas or Chicanos.
    I do not doubt that my study of Chicanas, of people of color and of racism in the United States is informed, but I have feared that my *gringa* name alone will cause a problem with my credibility. Biologically, I do not have any Chicana blood, but I believe I do, spiritually. Really, I believe I am, to use Denise Chávez's words, "an intuitive gringa" (*Loving Pedro Infante* 9), hence the reason I feel comfortable writing about this subject. Likewise, as Chicana author and painter Raquel Valle-Sentíes once told

me during an instant message session on America On-Line, "I think you were a Chicana in another life."

It is my hope that through this work, my years of research, the interviews with the six Chicana (and 1 Latina) *artistas* discussed herein and my simple passion for the plight of the Chicana, I will produce a work in which many people will read and appreciate for not only its content but also for the message it delivers. I hope that the interviews will encourage members inside and outside the Chican@ community to read and explore the work of these and other Chicana artists. This work will be beneficial because it will give people a better understanding of the plight of the Chicana in the United States—what she has gone through and how she survives. I believe through social awareness, social situations and conditions can be changed. I anticipate that in a small but important way the Chicana's position in today's society can be improved through this work.

With that said, this work concerns the literature and film that came out of the Chicana Movement and the Chicanisma it produced. During the Chicano Movement (the 1960s and the 1970s), Chicanas helped Chicanos achieve equal rights in the United States, while at the same time suffering their own oppression as women in their own race. Once Chicanas became fully aware that their interests were not being represented by their brothers nor being acknowledged by the feminist movement (that was dominated by Anglo women with Anglo interests) of the 1970s, Chicanas began their own movement, the Chicana Feminist Movement, that addressed the specific needs of Chicanas as women of color in the United States.

With the onset of that movement, artistic Chicanas sprang up everywhere—in film, in literature, in music and in many other venues. Chicana artists found that expressing themselves through these venues, they were able to confront the triple oppression they faced in

American society—that of race, class and gender. Confronting this oppression, a sense of Chicanisma arose. Or the sense of sisterhood and feminist discourse that emerged during the Chicana Movement and thereafter. With Chicanisma, Chicana artists (writers and filmmakers alike) began to write and produce artistic works in which Chicanas were given a just name, voice and image (something that many historical texts and other artistic works had denied them).

Six such works that display Chicanisma are: *Chicana* (a film by Sylvia Morales), *Puppet: A Chicano Novella* (a book by Margarita Cota-Cárdenas), *La Ofrenda: The Days of the Dead* (a film by Lourdes Portillo and Susana Muñoz), *Paletitas de Guayaba* (a book by Erlinda Gonzáles-Berry), *El Espejo/The Mirror* (a film by Frances Salomé España) and *Loving Pedro Infante* (a book by Denise Chávez). These six works, that collectively represent a period of 20 years in history, are for, by and about Chicanas$_{12337}$. However, they are not limited to a Chicana audience. Yes, they are for Chicanas, but they are also for the larger American, Mexican and global community. They all (re)discover and (re)present history and in so doing give Chicanas a rightful name, image and voice, not only in the eyes of Chicanas, but also in the eyes of Chicanos, mexicanos, Anglos, everyone! By (re)discovering and (re)presenting history and culture, these films and novellas demystify masculine power by confronting and battling the oppression Chicanas have received for years. In fact, by addressing race, gender and class issues through literature and film, Chicana writers and filmmakers finally give a voice to the voiceless and offer a more realistic look into historical, cultural and societal portrayals of the Chicana experience.

In many ways, to label the group of artists discussed herein is not necessarily fair, because in reality they all have multiple identities that are constantly changing. For example, Erlinda Gonzáles-Berry identifies primarily as a *nuevamejicana*, whereas Denise Chávez sees herself as a mejicana in the primary sense (but, Denise does not like labels). They also see themselves as Chicanas and Latinas (Denise also identifies as a nuevamejicana), but on different levels than their primary level. As Erlinda Gonzáles-Berry states, "My ethnic identity is multiple, fluid and strategic" (Personal Interview 5/7/04). Meaning of course, that the label of Chicana is truly one of convenience when talking about this group of six women, yet at the same time it does apply on one level or another. While all these women identify as Chicanas at some level, they have other identities, and it is important to keep this in mind while reading this work.

In this book, these six works are discussed and examined individually to see how each work exhibits examples of Chicanisma. The works are discussed chronologically beginning with Sylvia Morales' film, *Chicana*, in 1979 and ending with Denise Chávez's *Loving Pedro Infante* in 2001. Although it was not meant to work out this way, the works are discussed in the parallel pattern of film, book, film, book and so on.

Chapters two through four discuss, first the word Chican@, second, Racism in American society and the Chicana and third, the Chicana Movement and the emergence of Chicanisma. Following these introductory chapters the six works are discussed and are then followed by a conclusion. In the appendices, the full text of the interviews with each author and filmmaker can be found. However, I have copied parts of their interviews and included them in the discussion of their respective work.

The interviews with the authors/filmmakers were conducted in different ways. I had (recorded) phone conversations with Denise Chávez, Sylvia Morales and Lourdes Portillo and later transcribed the interviews. Margarita Cota-Cárdenas, Frances Salomé España and Erlinda Gonzáles-Berry chose to answer my questions through e-mail. Susana Muñoz, who resides in Argentina, and I corresponded through regular mail—I sent her questions, and she sent me her answers. All the interviews were followed up by further questions through e-mail, yet the major portion of the interviews were completed in the respective ways mentioned above.

Chapter 2
Chican@: What's in a Word?

*Chicana, Pocha, Tex-Mex,
Mexican-American, Hispanic.
So many labels.
Which one should I use?*
—Raquel Valle Sentíes
from the poem, "Growing Up *En Laredo*"

Acquiring an accurate idea of one's identity is a struggle few conquer. Therefore, it is no surprise that identity-recognizing terms also a struggle to understand. One such term is Chican@$_{12338}$. Simply put, a Chican@ is an American man or woman of Mexican descent. Yet, this definition does not convey the complexity of the term. The word's complexity is best understood through examination of the term—by contrasting it to other terms used for people of Mexican descent, and by looking at the origin of the word, its political value, its self-identifying value and ultimately coming to a complete understanding of it.

Distinguishing Chican@ from terms like, Hispanic, Latin@ and Mexican-American, will help explain the differences between these often misused and misunderstood words. Hispanic and Latin@ are terms that are often misapplied and used as a way to describe a race of a people$_{12339}$. These terms Latin@ and Hispanic identify ethnicity not race. Hispanic, more specifically, "connotes a lineage or cultural heritage related to Spain" (Robles 1). Yet, many Hispanics are not of Spanish origin, but rather have African lineage or indigenous roots or a combination of the two or all three. According to Muñoz,

Hispanic was founded "in the corridors of the federal bureaucracy and in the offices of the four Mexican American and one Puerto Rican member of Congress after the decline of the Chicano Movement" (10). Hispanic was established in the 1970s in the United States to lump together various groups of people for the 1980 census: "[r]ealizing that among the U.S. minorities it had seriously undercounted in the 1970 census were people of Latin-American extraction, the bureau [...] launched a campaign to help it get a better head count in 1980" (Del Olmo 9). Therefore, Hispanic incorporated people of Puerto Rican, Cuban, Mexican, Central and South American descent or other Spanish culture of origin. Because the term incorporated class, race, ethnicity and language differences and because it labeled and lumped together a diverse group of people, it was derogatory. Muñoz makes this more explicit:

> The term Hispanic reflects a continued politics of white ethnic identity, which de-emphasizes, if it does not reject, the Mexican cultural base of the people [...] it ignores the complexities of a multitude of different cultural groups, each with its own unique history, class realities, and experience in the United States...[it] complicated the question of identity for each of the groups it includes [...] It implicitly emphasizes the white European culture of Spain at the expense of the nonwhite cultures that have profoundly shaped the experiences of all Latin Americans. (Muñoz 10-11)

For these reasons, the term Hispanic has been rejected by Chican@s, Latin@s as an identifying term. Yet, at the same time, the lack of common identity of this group of people because of class, race, ethnicity and language differences is one of their unifying factors. This lack of common identity manifested itself in the term Latin@. Cartoonists, like Lalo Alcaraz, have made light of these different terms (Figure 1).

LA CUCARACHA ©2003 Lalo Alcaraz. Dist. By UNIVERSAL PRESS SYNDICATE. Reprinted with permission. All rights reserved.

Figure 1. La Cucaracha 8/24/03 by Lalo Alcaraz

Like Chican@, Latin@$_{12340}$ is a term people have chosen for themselves for it refers more to a geographical location and to languages spoken by people from that location. When considering why the term is used today, Del Olmo argues:

> It could be simply that the word Latino rolls more easily off the tongue of Spanish-speakers than an English word like Hispanic. Maybe if the Census Bureau had used the Spanish word Hispano in 1980, rather than Hispanic, this whole argument would be moot. (10)

Regardless of its origin of use, an argument remains between the terms. Ultimately, both Hispanic and Latino are all-encompassing terms with various subcategories, including Chican@. In other words, a Chican@ can be a Hispanic or a Latin@, but a Hispanic or Latin@ is not necessarily Chican@.

Mexican-American can be more or less paralleled with

the term of Chican@, yet it is an older term—one that was more widely used before Chican@, and still today it is often used over Chican@ because it does not carry a political connotation like Chican@. Mexican-American surfaced during the 1940s because World War II instilled a sense of patriotism in people of Mexican descent residing in the United States. Yet, Mexican-American was imposed on them from American society and as the years passed the young militants of Mexican descent of the 1960s did not want to be referred to as another hyphenated group in American society. Therefore, they looked for another term from which they could create their/an identity. This term was Chican@. In *The Chicano Experience*, Mirandé mentions that many use Chican@ to avoid being labeled by the U.S. government:

> The pervasive use of "Mexican-American," for example, fails to recognize that "Chicano" is a word self-consciously selected by many persons as symbolic of positive identification with a unique cultural heritage. Many have not realized that Mexican-American is analogous to Negro or colored, whereas Chicano is analogous to black. Both terms denote persons of Mexican extraction living in the United States, but they have very different connotations. (3)

As Mirandé suggests and as Del Olmo confirms: "[i]t was "our" word [...] It emerged form the barrio, and was not a label imposed on us by outside society, like Mexican-American (or, later on, Hispanic)" (11).

Although its wide use began in the 1960s, Chican@'s origins began earlier than the 1960s. No one author seems to know the true origin of the word "Chicano." Many have said the word originates from the word "Mexicano," "the word used in Mexico today to refer to the 1.5 million people who still speak Nahuatl (Aztec)" (Durán and Bernard 3). Many authors concur that the word comes from an indigenous language. According to Susan Rinderle, the term came from a Nahuatl pronunciation of the word, "*Mexicano*."

Some say that the word comes from "the indigenous Nahuatl-origin word *mexicano* with a Nahuatl, not Spanish, pronunciation. Some Chican@s therefore spell it with an "X" ("Xican@"—similar pronunciation) to further emphasize their indigenous roots. Others say it was formed as a conscious identification with laborers and farm workers—as a co-opting of a derogatory term. (Rinderle 18)

John Chávez in his classic book, *The Lost Land*, also mentions that the term emphasized the indigenous roots of the group:

> The use of the term "Chicano," derived from *mexicano* and formerly used disparagingly in referring to lower-class Mexican-Americans, signified a renewed pride in the Indian and mestizo poor who had built so much of the Southwest during the Spanish and Anglo colonizations. (130)

Del Olmo suggests that the origin of the word might be a result of several factors:

The consensus among Mexican-American scholars is that Chicano is a slang word that first came into wide use in the Southwest early in the 20th Century. It referred to Mexicans residing in the United States either as citizens or refugees from the Mexican Revolution of 1910 and the two decades of political chaos that followed. One theory of the word's derivation is that it is a combination of Chihuahua and Mexicano. And, indeed, most of the Mexicans who entered this country during that era did so at what was then the chief railroad junction on the border—El Paso, Texas, just across the Rio Grande from the Mexican state of Chihuahua. [...] By the 1940s and '50s, the word was widely used in barrios from San Antonio's West Side to East L.A., mainly by young hipsters known as pachucos. Because it was closely associated with rebellious, and sometimes criminal, youngsters, respectable Mexican Americans did not start using the term until the highly politicized 1960s. (11)

In *Chicana: The Mexican-American Woman*, Alfred Mirandé and Evangelina Enríquez also mention that the word may stem from the word "Mexicano", yet they go a step further, explaining that it might have origins even deeper than "Mexicano:"

> Some argue that its origins are ancient, deriving from the Nahuatl for "Mexican" or "Aztec." A less elevated but perhaps more plausible interpretation is that it is a distorted or americanized version of "mexicano." The Chicano, like a *pocho*, was a tainted or contaminated *mexicano*. The word seems to have has a paradoxical meaning like "nigger" or "queer," pejorative when used by outsiders and positive when used by insiders. Significantly, it is a term that had been adopted by Chicanos themselves. Just as black Americans selected "black," a previously pejorative term, as the rallying point for the black movement, and as a source of pride and dignity, so Chicanos have self-consciously chosen Chicano. (Mirandé and Enríquez 10-11)

Regardless of its true origin, the fact remains that the term was adopted by Chican@s for Chican@s. However, this adoption has not necessarily clarified the meaning of the term.

In fact, Chican@ is so difficult for people to fully

understand that many writers have felt the need to justify the use of the term or to define it in their works. For example, Mirandé and Enríquez state:

> We will use the term "Chicana" to denote a woman of Mexican ancestry living in the United States, whether she refers to herself as Mexican, Mexican-American, *latina*, *hispana*, or whatever. However, we do not wish to suggest that Chicanas are homogenous or uniform, for there is a great diversity among them. In terms of ethnic identity they range from those who see themselves as *mexicanas*, even though raised and perhaps born in the United States, to those who see themselves as "Americans" [...] Similarly, some Chicanas are bilingual while others are monolingual, either in English or Spanish. There are also generational differences. Third- and fourth-generation women tend to become more Americanized, although many, especially, the college educated, are rediscovering their Mexican-Indian roots. (11)

Later in their introduction they make a more concise definition of the word using a list of four categories: "The Chicana is a woman (1) of Mexican descent, (2) living in the United States, (3) culturally neither Mexican nor American but influenced by both societies, and (4) from a colonized minority" (Mirandé and Enríquez 12). Authors like Clare Mar-Molinero use the term Chicano while writing and simply put: "*Latinos* of Mexican-origin" (185) in parenthesis to quickly define the term. Other authors, like Domínguez, feel compelled to define Chicana before using it as a part of their work:

> For the purposes of this book, Chicana is defined as any of the following: 1) U.S. born of Mexican descent, 2) Mexican born, but raised

primarily in the United States, or 3) Mexican immigrant "naturalized" to the United States through long-term residency. The term Chicana, then, is directly related to the specific social context of the United States but is also formulated in resistance, as social activism, to that context and the roles therein defined. The term Chicana should be considered and recognized as both a self-given identity and an innately political one, connoting a specific orientation to the social and political body of dominant society. (121)

Galindo and Gonzáles, editors of *Speaking Chicana*, also feel the need to define the term:
> For the purpose of this book, "Chicana" is defined as someone born in the United States or who migrated to the United States; someone who has cultural and linguistic contact with two cultures and who may have experienced the "crossings of borders" as described by Anzaldúa (1987). (4)

Interestingly, while Galindo and Gonzáles use the feminine version of the word, they never designate the feminine, but rather use the neutral "someone". Perhaps this is because Chicanos have nearly everything in common with the Chicanas, but their sex. Quite literally, "Chicana" is the feminine form of the word "Chicano"— following the basic masculine/feminine rules of the Spanish language. "Chicana" with an ending "a", designates the feminine gender. Yet, unlike their brothers, Chicanas have a third oppression—that of gender. As women they suffer from a triple oppression (race, class and gender), whereas their men suffer a double oppression: race and class. This aspect of the Chicana is critical to acknowledge when speaking of her[1,2,3,4].

Many argue that Chican@ is political because Chican@ came out of the Chicano Movement of the 1960s. As Rinderle suggests, "[s]ince 'Chicano' was a political identity instead of a racial or ethnic identity, it was not an identity necessarily accepted by the wider Mexican-origin community" (19). In fact, many Mexicans do not identify with Chicanos because "Chicanos are traitors: they are the Mexicans who left and never looked back, the ones who put themselves, their ambitions, before everyone else" (Mathiessen xiii). Clearly, this quote refers to those Mexicans (or the children of Mexicans) that crossed the U.S.-Mexico border looking for a better way of life and eventually acculturating into American society. Robles explains this further:

> The term "Chicano" to Mexicans from Mexico carries a negative connotation too. Chicanos are seen as "pochos" (the term Pocho is used to identify a Mexican who has become agringad@ —too yankeedied—a wannabe American). Chicanos are seen as someone corrupted by Anglo culture. He's seen as an in-between-person not accepted by his own people because he has become something of a traitor. (1)

Yet, Chican@ can also refer to someone whose parents or grandparents lived in New Mexico, for example, when it was still a part of Mexico before the United States acquired the territory in 1848. Because of this disparity between how a Chican@ is of Mexican origin (that is, if their ancestors were border crossers or of original New Mexicans) there are regional variations of the definition of the word, as well. These variations are usually political.

As Robles explains: "[e]ven though the term 'Chicano' has now come into widespread usage, the term still retains unsavory connotation to some people, particularly because it's still preferred by political activists and reflects an anti-Anglo view" (1). Rubén Salazar also mentions this fact: "a Chicano is a Mexican-American with a non-Anglo image of himself" (7). These political, anti-Anglo connotations come from the initial usage of the term during the Chicano Movement.[12342] *Youth, Identity, Power: The Chicano Movement*, Carlos Muñoz expresses his frustration of the widespread usage of the word:

> The term Chicano has been applied uncritically by both Mexican American scholars and political activists since it was popularized in the late 1960s. It has come to mean simply those who are of Mexican descent, whether born in the United States or in Mexico. The political and ideological significance attached to the term by the founders of the Chicano movement has been largely lost or modified to fit contemporary political struggles. (Muñoz 7)

Muñoz, a key figure in the Chicano Movement, grieves over its widespread usage and the loss of its original meaning—that is, a person of Mexican origin politicized about civil rights[12343]. Tafolla agrees that "...the history and the folklore of the word is not as relevant as what it means to those who presently use it" (Tafolla 6). Yet, Del Olmo conveys that "[a] key reason the use of the word Chicano persists is that the young militants who started using it in the 1960s are now middle-aged and middle-class" (12). Really, it comes down to the fact that Chican@ is a self-identifying term. People use it because it is what they have elected as a term with which they would like to identify.

In *Feminism on the Border: Chicana Gender Politics and Literature*, Salivar-Hull mentions that Chicana is "a self-representation that underscores her multiple subjectivity: the complex inextricability of race, class, and gender" (23). Identifying oneself as Chican@ is a subjective thing—it ultimately lies with the person and how s/he positions her/himself in society.

Many Chican@s have written poetry, songs and literature using the term Chican@. One such Chicano is the musician, Lalo Guerrero. Guerrero, born in Arizona to Mexican parents, wrote the song *El Chicano* in 1977 (he recorded it in the same year). The song (Appendix A) sums up the discussion well and also offers insight into its self-identifying factor. According to Guerrero, ultimately Chican@ is a positive term used by people who are proud of their heritage as Mexicans ("...la sangre que llevo/Es la de Benito Juárez"). As a group they share dual oppression of race and class. They are marginalized and discriminated against by both whites ("*Los gringos me discriminan/Como si fuera extranjero/A pesar de que esta tierra /Fué de México primero*") and Mexicans on the other side of the border ("*Para México soy pocho/No me aceptan mis hermanos*"). Yet, they fight for justice ("*Luchamos por la justicia/Para todo el Mexicano*") for all Mexicans—in the United States and in the world.

Chican@ is a complex term. Often the exact definition lies within the person self-identifying as such. The term in many areas of the country and in many circles has a strong political connotation, whereas in other areas it means little more than an American of Mexican descent. Chican@ is not the same as Hispanic, Latino and/or Mexican-American, as it is used more specifically to define a group of people of Mexican descent that do not want to be labeled by the U.S. government or by whites. While the origin of the word is uncertain, what is certain is that Chican@ is a term self-selected by Chican@s that exemplifies a social and political relationship with the dominant society and expresses cultural pride of heritage.

For the purpose of this book, by using the term Chicana, focus is immediately placed on the woman. In this context, Chicanas are, basically, women of Mexican origin or descent and/or who identify themselves as such because of their political and social relationship to the dominant society.

Chapter 3
Racism in American Society and the Chicana

How many years can some people exist,
before they're allowed to be free...
How many times can a man turn his head
and pretend that he just doesn't see...
—Peter, Paul and Mary

Chicanas over the last 150 years (basically ever since the signing of The Treaty of Guadalupe in 1848) have been oppressed by race, class and gender in American society. As a triple-oppressed woman, the Chicana is not part of American culture or Mexican culture; rather she is constantly crossing between these two cultures. While crossing the borders between American and Mexican culture she continues to live within an internally colonized society. In order to understand this, an examination of the historical, social and political position of Chicanas in American society is necessary. It is important to understand that these three positions of Chicanas are not separate positions, but one Chicana position in a society that has three aspects.

During the Chicano Movement of the 1960s, Chicanas were torn between supporting Chicano men and the Chicano Movement and the Women's Liberation Movement[1,2,3,4]—yet at the same time not fitting into either. Their fight for liberation within the Chicano Movement, the Women's Liberation Movement and the larger American society began with spreading consciousness through literature—books, speeches, essays, letters, articles and novels were written and eventually distributed. Being able to write books and articles, do critical analysis, make films—all things that were denied to their mothers (and fathers for the most part)—were liberating acts for Chicanas. Through writing, Chicanas were (and still are) able to express the social injustices they suffered. Since (or perhaps even before) American colonialism of the Southwestern United States, language and sexuality of Chicana women have been oppressed as a result of the domination of masculine discourses, Anglo-dominated society and institutionalized religion and state. Through their literature as well as via the National Conferences during the Chicana Movement, Chicanas began to bring socio-political awareness of their position in society.

Understanding ethnic and gender identities and how they crisscross is critical to understanding the Chicana position in society (Domínguez 121). Really, a Chicana's ethnic identity is the same as her racial identity. In other words, since race is a social construction imposed on groups by American society, we must understand how Chicanas and Chicanos are classified as such. Classically, American society groups an individual in a certain race according to the color of his/her skin color. Likewise, an individual can be grouped into an ethnic/racial category because of the combination of, but certainly not limited to: his/her religion, language, national origin and/or cultural differences. However, these categories are really categories that define or set-off one's ethnicity (Better 19). Therefore, Chicanas are racially oppressed within the category of race, yet they are ethnically oppressed as well. Because of their racial and ethnic oppression, socially and politically they are internally colonized within American society.

The internal colonial theory was initially observed by

sociologist, Robert Blauner whilst studying the victimized condition of the African American in this country.[1,2,3,4,5] He explored the thesis that the relationship between whites and African Americans in this country was one of the colonizer and the colonized (393). In other words, the American racial conflict can be viewed in terms of a colonial analogy:

> [T]he United States operates an internal colony through its economic and political domination of ethnic enclaves: ghettos, Indian reservations, barrios and Chinatowns. These enclaves are closely patrolled by local law enforcement organizations. The inhabitants have little voice in the functioning of their communities or the society at large. (Better 9)

Of course, the internal colonial theory is directly related to the idea of neocolonialism—the idea that the economic and political policies implemented by a greater power are indirectly put into action to maintain or extend influence over areas or people (Better 9). In other words, within one nation (for us, the United States) there is still a "Mother Country" that operates within that country. The Chican@ barrio becomes the colony within its own country and the mother country is Anglo domination and influence over that Chican@ barrio. Tomás Almaguer explains this further in his article, *Historical Notes on Chicano Oppression: The Dialectics of Racial and Class Domination in North America*:

> U.S. Colonization of the Mexicano was carried out "internally" [...] What occurred to the Mexicano in the Southwestern Unites States was a reflection of the very same forces that were at work in the establishment of overseas or external colonial relations. The "annexation" of the land and natural resources of Northern México and

the proletarianization of an exploitable Mexican labor force were to contribute four major elements to the development and stabilization of U.S. capitalism. (41)

Neocolonialism exists so that the dominating and ruling class can maintain its supremacy in society. For the Chicana, neocolonialism[12346] is the economic and political policies that white America establishes to indirectly control them and their community. Mirandé and Enríquez speak further of the internal colonialism model, and its relation to the Chicana in their book, *La Chicana: The Mexican-American Woman*. When the Southwest was conquered by Anglos, internal colonialism began. Chican@s "...constitute an internal colony within the territorial boundaries of the United States" (Mirandé and Enríquez 9). According to Barrea, "Internal colonialism means that Chicanos as a cultural/racial group exist in an exploited condition" (485). In the United States, Chican@s exist in a society where they are powerless, the result of capitalism. Chican@ businesses are typically owned by outsiders and other institutions are controlled by outsiders—hence preventing Chican@ direct control. The informal existence and subtleness of internal colonialism makes it difficult to identify, and therefore forcing Chican@s to remain in subordinate roles within American society. This is where Chican@ class oppression exists. As Mirandé and Enríquez reiterate, "The internal colony is a de facto one, with formal and legal equality but informally executed from the legal-political system" (9).

As internally colonized women, Chicanas are constantly crossing borders, a concept that was initially discussed by Gloria Anzaldúa in her timeless work, *Borderlands/La Frontera: The New Mestiza*. In it, she discusses crossing psychological borderlands, sexual borderlands and spiritual borderlands. She says:

> . . .the Borderlands are physically present wherever two or more cultures edge each other, where people of different races occupy the same territory, where under, lower, middle and upper classes touch, where the space between two individuals shrinks with intimacy. (19)

Because the Chicana lives literally on the border of these "Borderlands", she is not fully a member of one or another, yet a combination of both. Mirandé and Enríquez claim:

> [T]he essence of being Chicana is that one is not fully Mexican or American. [Yet] [i]nternal colonization means that Chicanas are free to be Mexican and American but not Chicana, since Chicanos are a nonentity in colonial America. In other words, she may be Mexican (i.e., foreign) or American—a noncolonized non-Chicana. (12)

As a woman who understands both cultures, she crosses these borders in her daily encounters. For example, she crosses borders when she speaks Spanish in one place (or in one moment) and English in another (assuming, of course, that she is a bilingual Chicana). Beyond linguistic borders, she also crosses social and cultural borders—accommodating and acculturating to the situation when and where necessary. In *The Chicana and the Women's Rights Movement*, Consuelo Nieto states, "As a bicultural person, [the Chicana] participates in two worlds, integrating her Mexican heritage with that of the majority society" (10). The Chicana continually operates in these two worlds, yet never feels a part of either. The Chicana's lack of acceptance can be understood under the context of American society, as they are internally colonized by Chicanos and by whites. In *Twice a Minority:*

Mexican American Women, Margarita Melville states: "Mexican American women, as Mexican Americans, are a minority population...in their relationship to Anglo American society... [and] possess a minority status in relation to their own brothers and husbands...[t]hey are twice a minority" (2). These two social structures, Anglo American society and Chicano society, define Chicanas as people of color and as women.

Like Chicanos, Chicanas are colonized by Anglo-American society. Yet unlike Chicanos, Chicanas have been internally colonized within Chicano culture through the Catholic Church and the Chicano family. Ana Castillo in her *Massacre of the Dreamers* explains the role the Catholic Church has played in Chicanas' lives:

> The Catholic Church as an institution supported by the Mexican community in the U.S. seems to be a cultural norm rather than a source for real spiritual comfort [...] it is the church that represent authority in her [the Chicana's] life, especially over her sexuality and reproductive ability. (48)

As stated earlier, certain cultural icons are imposed by the Chicano community to impose traditional gender roles on Chicanas. In fact, the cultural icons are usually related to the Catholic Church. The Church, which was initially forced on the Chican@ community by the Spaniards (Europeans) before the Southwestern United States (or the Mexican north) belonged to the United States, enforced its male-dominated ideology and power structure through the male-orientated god that it worshiped. Equally Catholic icons like the Virgin Mary (nowadays, known as *La Virgen de Guadalupe* within the Chicano community) became role models for Chicanas—the Virgen de Guadalupe as a role model oppressed Chicanas not only as sexual beings, but also as women because icons like the Virgin Mary emphasized women's reproductive responsibility as breeders. Additionally, women within the Catholic Church were portrayed as "submissive, chaste and unworldly" (Martínez and McCaughan 51). This ideology perpetuated Chicanas gender and sexual marginalization.

Of course, once Mexico's northern territory was acquired by the United States, religious organizations and social institutions began the assimilation, acculturation and Americanization process of the Chicano people. In fact, Mirandé and Enríquez note that the colonization of the American Southwest and the conquest of Mexico are remarkably similar (8-9). Slowly, but surely, Chican@s were stripped of their language (Spanish[12347]) and acculturated into American society—reading, writing and speaking in English, saluting the American flag, eating American food, etc. While learning these American cultural values, Chicanas learned that they held a subservient position in society not only to the Anglo American male, but also to the Chicano. In *Hijas de Cuahtemoc*, a Chicana newspaper that came out of the Chicana Movement, Dorinda Moreno Gladden expresses that :

> The church has worked to hinder and oppress the woman in many ways. It has taught the woman that she must suffer in order to get closer to god [...] The Church has oppressed [sic] her by defining and limiting her role. Such phrases as *Hija de La Chingada, Hija de Malinche*, and *Hija de María* are examples of this. The Church has supported the necessity to keep the woman ignorant, barefoot and pregnant by condemning legal abortions and birth control. (2)

As this quote subtly suggests, in Chican@ culture the Church and the family are interrelated. Consuelo Nieto also notes that when considering the history of Chicanas, the role of the Catholic Church is an important one:

> Not all Chicanos are Catholic, and among those who belong to the church, not all participate actively. But since the arrival of the Spanish, the values, traditions, and social institutions of the Church have been tightly interwoven in Chicano family life. (10-11)

Actually, the patriarchy of the Chicano Movement really came out of the Chicano family that emphasized a hierarchical structure according to masculinity. According to Mirandé and Enríquez:

> The family is undoubtedly the most important institution for Chicanos, and the woman in turn is the backbone of the culture. Although the woman is largely relegated to the home, her domestic role is not passive. She is charged with essential familial functions: reproduction of the species, transmission of cultural values and beliefs to the next generation, and provision of needed warmth, support, and affection for family members who must survive in a hostile environment. (116)

However, as they later observe:

> [A]lthough the Chicano family is ostensibly patriarchal, it is in fact mother centered...Men have power and authority relative to outside institutions, and women are responsible for the daily affairs of the family...with each granted power and authority within their respective spheres. (117)

Chicanas operate in the private sphere, whereas Chicanos operate in the public sphere. Traditionally,

Chicanas as women (as maternal figures) have been relegated to the home. Yet, as mothers, Chicanas are traditionally responsible for passing on cultural values to future generations. Because of this responsibility, they do have the ability to perpetuate the patriarchal ideas of the family. This happens especially if they are not fully aware of their inferior position in Chican@ society and the larger American society. As oppressed people, the perpetual state of oppression will continue, unless education is there to break the cycle/mode. There are those Chicanas who have been educated about the oppressive role Chicanas occupy within and outside Chican@ culture and these Chicanas are slowly, but surely educating their sons and daughters about *her*story rather *his*story.

Her story includes exposing the subordinate role in which the family and the Church have sought to maintain the Chicana. The Chicano family and the Catholic Church have kept Chicanas in subordinate roles. Mirta Vidal in *Chicanas Speak Out: Women: New Voice of La Raza* claimed that during the Chicano Movement when men appealed for unity of *La Raza* (because unity "is the basic foundation of the Chicano Movement" (8), they were maintaining women's subordinate position in the family. "[W]hen Chicano men talk about maintaining La Familia and the "cultural heritage" of *La Raza*, they are in fact talking about maintaining the age-old concept of keeping the woman barefoot, pregnant, and in the kitchen" (8). In fact, fighting the subordination of the Chicana through the Chican@ family was a crucial issue for Chicanas during the Chicana Movement:

> We have to fight a lot of Catholic ideas in our homes and in the movement. For example, the idea of large families is very Catholic. The Pope says no birth control, abortions, lots of kids (and make me richer). So what do the guys say in the

movement, have lots of kids, keep up the traditional chicano [sic] family. ("*El Movimiento and the Chicana*" 41-42)

As seen by the frustration in this woman's voice during the movement, the Catholic Church and the Chicano family are oppressive forces that are interrelated and that impose subordination of the Chicana. Of course, the concept of a large Catholic family also ties in with the socio-economic oppression Chicanas face. Because Chicanas are pressured to have large families, they often fall victims to welfare. If they are not victims of welfare, then they are most certainly living without the excess funds to allow them to save and invest; and consequently they do not have the opportunity to acquire economic success in American society.

In conclusion, Chicanas are triple oppressed women in the United States. Because of this oppression, they are an internally colonized people and must be understood within this context. Their triple oppression of race, class and gender are constantly overlapping and intertwining—making for a complex woman of color who cannot be understood within a specific framework. According to Sandra Ugarte, in *Hijas de Cuahtemoc*, "There is class, race and women's oppression which is tied into the same thing—capitalism. We cannot just separate these types of oppression and leave them separated" (2). Because these types of oppression cannot be separated, they all need to be addressed for the total liberation for Chicanas.

Chapter 4
The Chicana Movement and the Emergence of Chicanisma

Women may develop a feminist consciousness as a result of their experiences with sexism in revolutionary struggles or mass social movements
  —Shelia Rowbotham

Arising from the Chicano Movement and the Women's Liberation Movement, the Chicana Movement grew out of the reaction to these movements and developed from the speeches, essays, letters, and articles published in Chican@ newspapers, journals and newsletters. Finding contradictions and dialectical opposition both in the Chicano Movement (which focused on racial problems rather than racial and gender problems) and the Women's Liberation Movement (that focused on the middle-class white women), the Chicana Movement addressed the specific needs of Chicanas as women of color in the United States. The Chicana feminist discourse, which resulted from the Movement, would address the issues of race, class and gender—the triple oppressions of the Chicana[1,2,3,4,8]. Like, Chicanismo, the cultural nationalism that arose during the Chicano Movement, Chicanisma[1,2,3,4,9] arose from the Chicana Movement. Acting like a domino effect, the Chicano Movement in combination with the Women's Liberation Movement (and other minority women's movements) led to the Chicana Movement and ultimately the concept of Chicanisma within Chican@ culture. This chapter illustrates how this occurred.

In the 1960s, Chicano workers began a fight against the oppression and discrimination that the Chicano community had (has) been subjected to since the signing of the Treaty of Guadalupe Hildalgo (February 2, 1848) ending the Mexican-American War.$_{1,2,3,50}$ The treaty's provisions called for Mexico to cede 55% of its territory to the U.S. (present-day Arizona, California, New Mexico, Texas, and parts of Colorado, Nevada and Utah, Wyoming and Kansas) in exchange for fifteen million dollars in compensation for war-related damage to Mexican property.

Nearly 100 years after the signing of the Treaty of Guadalupe Hildalgo, Chicano workers hoped their fight, which came to be known as the Chicano Movement, would lead to social justice and equality. The Chicano Movement really emerged out of the Civil Rights Movement that was already taking place in our country. Chicanos experienced segregation in schools and were not allowed to vote. Along with the African American Civil Rights Movement, the struggle for migrant farm workers' rights in the San Joaquín Valley in California was the catalyst of the Chicano Movement.

Commencing in the early 1960s, this struggle, known as *La causa*, was led by César Chávez and Dolores Huerta. Chávez was heavily influenced by the teachings of Ghandi and was a follower of Martin Luther King, Jr.; thus, he opted to follow a non-violence approach for the struggle, believing that such an approach would be effective in California. Effective it was—in 1969 Chávez, Dolores Huerta and their union, the UFW (United Farm Workers), were finally successful in getting the growers to sign a contract for migrant workers' rights. After the nation-wide grape boycott, enough economic pressure was put on the growers so that they had no other choice but to sit down and talk about worker's rights. The grape boycott became the heart and soul of the Chicano Movement because it represented the first time that Chican@s had organized together and been successful as a result.[12351] The very fact that Chican@s were out there taking a stand was an inspiration for all Chican@s. During the UFW's struggle, many students from nearby California universities and colleges came to the San Joaquin Valley to help with *La causa*. Many of these students were from working-class backgrounds, had agricultural roots and were the first members of their families to go to college; therefore as people who had more contact with the land and understood the working-class struggle, they were passionate about *La causa* and were willing to come and help.

Eventually, Chicano youths became interested in more than just migrant workers' rights. In 1969, the first Chicano Youth Conference was held. At this conference, Corky Gonzáles proposed that Chican@ people came from Aztlán. By establishing a common mythical homeland with Aztlán[12352], Gonzáles gave value to the Chicano existence—something that had been devalued by white people. In time, young Chicanos demanded to be taught their own culture and language. In effect, this new found Chicano cultural nationalism, Chicanismo, shared ideological roots with black cultural nationalism. According to Alma M. García, Professor of Sociology at Santa Clara University, Chicanismo

> ...advocated an ideology and spirit of active resistance within Mexican-American communities throughout the United States [...] [It] emphasized cultural pride as a source of political unity and strength capable of mobilizing Chicanos and Chicanas into an oppositional political group within the dominant political landscape in the United States. (3)

Ramón A. Gutiérrez explains this further in "*Community, Patriarchy and Individualism:*"
> "*Chicanismo* meant identifying with *La Raza* (the race of the people), and collectively promoting the interests of *carnales* (or brothers) with whom they shared a common language, culture, religion, and Aztec heritage" (588). In fact, the Chicano Movement and Chicanismo would concentrate on the Chicano, denying recognition of the Chicana and her issues as a woman. In this Chicano Movement for equality, the Chicana found herself in an inferior position.

Although Chicanas worked to gain equal status in a movement dominated by men, they stayed in subordinate roles. Actually, in the beginning of the Chicano movement, the active Chicanas "did not distinguish their empowerment as women from the empowerment of their families and communities" (Moya 63). As Chicanas fought for *La causa*, it was evident within the Chicano community that Chicanas had not and would not acquire gender equality because fundamentally the movement was about economic, educational and political equality. The movement was male-defined and Chicano nationalists wanted to keep it that way.

Chicanas were put in subordinate positions, not in leadership positions within the Chicano Movement. "Within the Chicano Student Movement, women were denied leadership roles and were asked to perform only the most traditional stereotypical roles—cleaning up, making coffee, executing the orders men gave, and servicing their needs" (Gutiérrez 589). As long as Chicanas supported men in the fight for men's civil rights they were not a problem, however once they mentioned gender issues along with racial issues they were not accepted. Due to the fact that Chicano nationalists were fearful of cultural genocide, they began to use Mexican cultural icons to remind Chicanas of their position in society:

> Chicano cultural nationalists had self-consciously taken up a series of Mexican cultural icons in order to project an alternative, and more affirming, Mexican/Chicano cultural reality. Among these three female icons—*La Virgen de Guadalupe*, La Malinche, and La Llorona—which taken together shape the boundaries of traditional Chicana womanhood. (64)

These three women, *La Virgen de Guadalupe*, La Malinche and La Llorona[12353], create the foundation of traditional gender roles, according to the norms of Mexican patriarchal society. In addition, Chicanas, who were raised in families where they were conscious of the traditional standards and values of the two cultural feminine icons, *La Virgen de Guadalupe* and La Malinche—two figures that were in dialectic opposition—were constantly reminded of their obligations to the church and to their family, without mentioning, of course, the severe double standard that supported the sexual liberty of men, but not of women.

In fact, during the UFW's *peregrinación* (pilgrimage) from Delano to Sacramento in 1966, the group was led by a banner with *La Virgen de Guadalupe* on it. As the patron saint of the Mexican people, *La Virgen* united *La Raza*. The original purpose of the banner was to show that Chican@s followed La Virgen, and not Karl Marx.[12354] While *La Virgen* helped to create a common cultural bond between the organizers, her symbolism was, in many ways negative for Chicanas. She was a constant reminder of the Chicana's obligation to Church and family. In effect, "...labels [such as *La Virgen de Guadalupe*] were often used as mechanisms of social control to discredit Chicanas who articulated a feminist political agenda" (Segura and

Pesquera 79). By perpetuating these historical myths during the Chicano movement, Chicanos were able to keep Chicanas in their traditional gender roles—allowing the men to continue to dominate the movement.

Likewise, the icon of La Malinche was oppressive for Chicanas. Gutiérrez explains this further:

> For activist Chicanas, the historical representations of Malinche as a treacherous whore who betrayed her own people were but profound reflections of the deep-seated misogynist beliefs in Mexican and Mexican American culture. The only public models open to Mexican women were those of the virgin and the whore. If women were going to go beyond them, then they had to begin by rehabilitating Malinche. (592)

So with the onset of the Chicana Movement, many Chicanas began to discover the truth about their past and about archetypal figures of their culture that suppressed them, like La Malinche. As they learned, La Malinche was not a sell-out to her people, but rather was sold by her own family to the Spanish. For this reason, many Chicana artists began to portray La Malinche in a new light, to eventually rid her of the horrible *"vendida"*—type falsified myth that she had acquired. Since the rights that Chicanas fought for were neither recognized nor honored in the Chicano movement in the late 1960s and early 1970s, Chicanas began to vocalize their disappointment of the gender discrimination within the movement. In fact, "Chicanas became increasingly vocal about their dissatisfaction at being expected to perform a disproportionate share of the work required for successful political organizing" (Moya 63). Angie Chabram-Dernersesian, Associate Professor of Chican@ Studies at the University of California at Davis, points out that:

> Textually within the very same Chicano vernacular which challenged the Eurolingocentrism of English and Spanish by crossing their borders in illegal codes that would elicit charges of "illiteracy," Chicano identity is written with linguistic qualifiers-*o/os*—which subsume the Chicana into a universal ethnic subject that speaks with the masculine instead of the feminine and embodies itself in a Chicano male. (82)

As a movement for equality, the Chicano movement was full of internal contradictions. Even within the Chicano vernacular, Chicanas were being denied recognition. Yet, Chicanas within the movement remained divided. In fact, the biggest conflict on women's issues was internal—among Chicanas.

Many Chicanas did not want to break from the struggle of the Chicano Movement, feeling that battling racism was more important than addressing feminist issues. For many Chicanas, race trumped gender. Many Chicanas thought they were denying their men loyalty within the movement if they broke from it and, instead, concentrated on Chicana issues. For this reason, these Chicanas were coined, "Loyalists" by Anna Nieto-Gómez, a Chicana feminist, in her article "La Feminista." Those Chicanas who saw the issues of sexism in the Chicano Movement as something that needed to be addressed alongside the matter of racism of the Chicano Movement were "Feministas". García explains how these women evolved as feministas:

> Many Chicanas, active within every sector of the movement, raised their voices in a collective feminist challenge to the sexism and male domination that they were experiencing within the movimiento. Developing first as cultural nationalists, these Chicanas began to see and

experience some of the contradictions of Chicanismo, specifically as it applied to women. From their nationalist base, these Chicana activists began to evolve also as feminists. ("*The Development of Chicana*" 3)

For many Chicana feminists, Chicana feminist thought sprang from the patriarchy and sexism at all levels of society and within the Chicano Movement:

> Chicana activists/feminists [. . .] shunned traditional roles and/or actively pursued Chicana-centered practices of resistance. [They] were the Chicanas who replaced the discourses of compadres and carnalismo with the discourses of *comadres* (sisters) and *feminismo* (feminists), macho with hembra, and fiercely combated male domination in the leadership of the Chicano Movement and the political life of the community. (Chabram-Dernersesian 84)

Feministas believed that racial equality could not be achieved if sexual equality was not realized. In fact, sexual oppression was seen as a huge obstacle towards the plight for the liberation of the Chicano people for many Chicanas. According to García, "Chicanas fought for gender equality always cognizant of the interplay between race/ethnicity and gender" (6).

Because of their position as women who wanted sexual equality along with racial equality and because they were not maintaining the interests of the Chicano Movement, they were often labeled as *vendidas* or "sell-outs." In fact, according to Anna Nieto-Gómez:

> From 1968-1971 feminism was rejected by the Chicano movement as irrelevant and anglo-inspired [...] the Chicana feminist ha[d] been cautioned to wait and fight for her cause at a later

time for fear of dividing the Chicano movement. Also it ha[d] been recommended that she melt into the melting pot of femaleness rather than divide the women's movement. (35)

With this in mind, Loyalists and Feminists did not see eye to eye and an intra-conflict/separation began with Chicanas:

> *Feministas* were viewed by the "Loyalists" as anti-family, anti-cultural, anti-man and therefore anti-Chicano movement. Women in search for identity, while developing a new role in society, could not be trusted. Searching for gender identity and sexual equality was an Anglo-bourgeois trip. "The "Loyalists" could only see the "Feministas" as ambitious, selfish women who were only concerned with themselves at the cost of everyone else." (35)

For this reason, many were labeled followers of white feminists and as lesbians (homosexuality, of course, coming in direct conflict with the preaching of the Catholic Church).

The disparity among the Chicanas lay in the fact that Chicanas grow up in an extremely patriarchal culture. As they struggled to break away from that culture, they found that speaking out against it was considered devaluing the Chicano people. Yet, ultimately, the awakening of Chicana consciousness was prompted by the *Machismo*[12356] of the movement as Nancy Nieto conveyed in one of the preliminary issues of *Hijas de Cuahtemoc*:

> When a freshman male comes to MECHA [Movimiento Estudiantil Chicano de Aztlán— a Chicano student organization in California] he is approached and welcomed. He is taught by observation that the Chicanas are only useful in areas of clerical and sexual activities.

When something must be done there is always a Chicana there to do the work. "It is her place and duty to stand behind and back up her Macho!". . .Another aspect of the MACHO attitude is their lack of respect for Chicanas. They play their games, plotting girl against girl for their own benefit. . .They use the movement and Chicanismo to take her to bed. And when she refuses, she is a vendida [sell-out] because she is not looking after the welfare of her men . . . Chicanos take the credit for the suggestions, the work and even the pride of a Chicana product. They take the credit without even a thank you to the workers. Chicanas are getting fed up with being told when to jump and how high. They are tired of being coerced to stay in their place or pay the price of losing a so-called boyfriend. Chicanas must be allowed to express themselves, to work for the movement and most of all, to accomplish something. (2)

As demonstrated within MECHA, clearly within the Chicano Movement, Chicanas were in subordinate roles because of the *Machismo* that dominated Chicano patriarchal society. However, in regards to this *Machismo*, there was an interesting counter viewpoint:

Machismo fits into the colonial mentality of the conqueror. It is a mechanism for shifting the focus away from Anglo oppression to alleged pathologies within Chicano culture. The universal oppression of women is ignored, and *Machismo* becomes a quaint custom practiced by Mexicans and Chicanos. It is as if the oppression of women is somehow peculiar to Mexican culture. Anglos fail to recognize that the Anglo women's movement was also motivated by male oppression—a reaction to white *Machismo*. (Mirandé and Enríquez 242)

In truth, Nieto's complaints of MECHA are frighteningly similar to the complaints of white and black women made during the Civil Rights Movement. In truth, the reason why the Women's Liberation Movement began is because of the *Machismo* of the Civil Rights Movement.

In fact, many Chicanas became interested in participating in the Women's Liberation Movement for this very reason. However, they soon discovered that they were ill-represented within the Women's Movement as well. After all, the Women's Liberation Movement was dominated by white women with white interests. Also known as the White Feminist Movement, Women's Liberation Movement concentrated on issues of the middle-class white women of the time—higher education, professional development, political agendas, etc. In fact, the women that benefited the most from the movement were the daughters of men in the corporate world. These men saw their daughters being denied opportunities, and therefore wanted to make a change to increase their daughter's opportunities. As Marta Cotera, a Chicana feminist, pointed out in a speech she gave in 1976:

> The issue of classism in the feminist ranks hit us square in the face. One fine day, we realized that Anglo feminists who were pulling certain "movidas" (moves) on us were not operating at the racist level [...] We realized that a certain air of arrogance, insensitivity to the needs or incomprehension of needs of poor women, regardless of race, come from another source. We realized that these feminists see all minority women as members of a certain class, mainly lower class. ("*Among the Feminists*" 217-218)

Because Chicanas were members of a lower class in society, they could not relate to the middle-class issues of the White Feminist Movement. As Domínguez points out:

> Chicanas as a social and political group occupy a precarious position in history. As members of the dominant society and their own Chicano community, Chicanas must be defined in terms of their ethnic identity, their gender identity, and the intersection of those identities [. . .] Chicanas' self-identities as people of color, women, and women of color are influenced by and subject to determinations from the dominant society and the Chicano community. Chicanas, as women and people of color, bordered two movements in the 1960s: the Chicano Movement and the Women's Movement. (120-121)

In reality, the Women's Liberation Movement could not relate nor was willing to relate to the plight of women of color for equal rights. In fact, Chicana feminists joined other feminist women of color in criticizing the movement's limited attention to differences among women on the basis of race, ethnicity, class and sexual orientation. Black women and Asian-American women also complained of their lack of representation in the Women's Liberation Movement (García 1989 220). Black, Asian-American and Native American women also formed their own organizations due to their lack of representation within the Women's Liberation Movement. Anna Nieto-Gómez addresses this: "...if women's issues do not address the language barriers, the cultural differences and class differences used to oppress women also, the women's movement can only represent one middle class, monolingual-monocultural vested interests" (43). Therefore, it came as no surprise that the Women's Liberation Movement did not appeal to the majority of Chicanas.

Ultimately, the lack of appeal of the Women's Liberation Movement and their lack of recognition in the Chicano Movement inspired Chicanas to begin their own movement: the Chicana Movement—a social movement that attempted to improve the position of Chicanas in "American" society and particularly addressed the specific issues affecting Chicanas as women of color in the United States. In May, 1971, the first National Chicana Conference was held in Houston, Texas. This conference brought Chicanas together from all over and clarified the confusion and disparity of attitudes towards the Chicana's position in the larger Chicano movement (Nieto-Gómez 35). In an effort to improve their position, goals were established. These goals included welfare rights, farm workers' rights, undocumented workers' rights, prisoners' rights, education rights, health care rights, legal rights, birth control rights, abortion rights and better working conditions. Likewise, Chicanas fought against the racial and sexual stereotypes thrown their way. Unlike their brothers, Chicanas did not want to exclude Chicanos from their movement. They realized that their movement needed to go beyond women's issues. After all, it would be hypocritical to be sexist like many Chicanos had been. Hence, the Chicana Movement was nationalist and feminist in its effort to improve the position of the Chicana in American society (García "The Development of Chicana Feminist..." 220). Many Chicanos did not support the movement, believing that it took away from the current Chicano Movement.

There were many Chicanas who had important roles during the Chicano Movement and who ultimately inspired the Chicana Movement—Alicia Escalante with the

Welfare Rights Organization, and Gracia Molina de Pick and Anna Nieto-Gómez[1,2,3,5,7] with feminist activities (Cotera "*Feminism: The Chicano*" 229). Yet, perhaps the most well-known woman and role model was/is Dolores Huerta, the then vice chairman of the UFW. As César Chávez's right hand *woman*, she was instrumental in the success of the UFW—her negotiations with the growers in the San Joaquín Valley won many battles for the UFW. As a Chicana leader, Huerta was aware of the importance of Chicanas in the Chicano Movement: "Look at our women. They are strong you can feel it. They are the rocks on which we really build" (García *Chicana Feminist Thought* 1). Women like Huerta would ultimately be inspirations to many Chicanas—especially Chicana artists who through these women found inspiration to express themselves creatively.

For example, many Chicanas began to write and publish speeches, essays, letters, articles, books and novels about the social injustices they experienced as a minority in American society. Alma M. García expresses how Chicana feminist discourse emerged in the 1970s through the 1980s:

> The years between 1970 and 1980 represented a formative period in the development of Chicana feminist thought in the United States. During this period, Chicana feminists addressed the specific issues affecting Chicanas as women of color in the United States. As a result of their collective efforts in struggling against racial, class, and gender oppression, Chicana feminists developed an ideological discourse that addresses three major issues. These were the relationship between Chicana feminism and the ideology of cultural nationalism, feminist baiting within the

Chicano movement, and the relationship between the Chicana feminist movement and the white feminist movement. (217)

In fact many publications addressed these three major issues: *Hijas de Cuahtemoc, Regeneración, Encuentro Femenil: The First Chicana Feminist Journal, La Comadre* and *Hembra*, just to name a few. These new publications, centered on the Chicana, allowed for a broader population base that could understand the plight of the Chicana. For example, in the first issue of the Chicana newspaper, published in 1971, *Hijas de Cuahtemoc* (Daughters of Cuahtemoc), Anna Nieto-Gómez called for an elimination of sexism in Chicano families and communities. Francisca Flores, the editor of the Chicana feminist publication, Regeneración, disputed that in the male-dominated Chicano movement, Chicanas could no longer be demoted to a subservient status. "Bernice Rincón argued that Chicana feminists, through their efforts to gain full equality for women, would strengthen El Movimiento by eradicating internal sources of oppression" (García 5). Chicanas believed that this eradication would occur through education. Yet, . . . there [was] no medium directly involved in educating La Chicana, not only of her history, but also of her role and importance in El Movimiento. [Therefore]. . . the purpose of the newspaper [*Hijas de Cuahtemoc*] [was] to encourage all Chicanas to express their ideas in as many ways as possible. ("Chicana Newspaper" 2)

Hijas de Cuahtemoc did encourage Chicanas to express themselves—by including many poems, illustrations and articles by, for and about Chicanas.

In addition to the new literature that sprang up to popularize the goals of the movement, regional and national conferences were held. These meetings were designed to draw attention to the most pressing needs of

Chicanas, such as welfare rights, reproductive rights, health care, poverty, immigration and education. The new periodicals of the movement, like *Hijas de Cuahtemoc*, not only advertised upcoming regional and national conferences by including the agendas of the meetings, but also articles in these periodicals covered the purposes of the conferences. Additionally, issues of *Hijas de Cuahtemoc* were distributed at the conferences—expanding their readership.

As the movement progressed, consciousness was spread as Chican@ Studies Departments at universities educated students about the plight of the Chicana. Additionally, many major Chicana feminist organizations arose to create opportunities for Chicanas. Some of them were the Chicana Service Action Committee (California), Mujeres Unidas (Colorado), Mexican-American Women National Association (MANA, Washington, D.C.), Mexican-American Business and Professional Women (Texas), Nacional Femenil (California), and the Mexican-American Women Political Caucus (Texas). Meanwhile, Chicana writers began to publish books and articles and Chicana filmmakers began to make films concentrating on Chicanisma nationalism.

While these consciousness raising efforts have changed Chicana consciousness, there is still a long way to go. The Chicana Movement's effort began in the 1970s, but continues today as Chicanas continue to struggle to have a powerful voice in American society. In fact, ". . .the Chicana [. . .] is still participating in the struggle for recognition and respect from white dominant society" (Castillo "*Massacre of Dreams*" 311).

The Chicana Movement that grew out of the Chicano Movement and the Women's Liberation Movement has surely made an impact on the lives of Chicanas. In many arenas, Chicanas now have a voice, an image and a name that they once did not have—where there was once a silence there is now a whisper. That voice, that image and that name arose from the commencement of their own struggle one that met their needs as women of color in the United States. Through the various forms of education, including the literature of the movement, books, essays, music, films and other printed material, Chicanisma emerged.

Chapter 5
Chicana (1979)

*Remembering, because the past is what
we have and it is all that we have.
It is from the past that we are able
to perceive, create and give
life of our ritual; it is from this
that we derive strength,
that we can recognize our existence
as human beings.*
—Tomás Rivera

Sylvia Morales' *Chicana*, an independent documentary film debuted at the beginning of the Chicana Feminist Movement in 1979. Many Chicanas chose to do documentaries to support the Chicana image within a historical and socio-cultural framework. Through documentary, filmmakers document history and culture, giving Chicanas the voice they have been denied in both American and Chicano film. It is understandable to see why Chicanas choose to produce documentaries, as "[t]he documentary form is still a very effective means of educating and reconstructing fact, truth and history" (Camplis 298). Liz Kotz in her article, "Unofficial Stories: Documentaries by Latinas and Latin American Women," claims that the attraction of a documentary for the woman filmmaker comes from the importance of documenting the reality, culture and perceptions of the underrepresented/ignored individuals in the dominant media (61). This is why Chicana filmmakers like Sylvia Morales and Lourdes Portillo (Chapter 7), address history and culture in their documental works—by revisiting facts, truth and history through documentation these filmmakers are able to finally give a rightful voice, image and name to the voiceless, imageless and nameless.

Chicana is a 22-minute film about Chicanas and their history. Morales first got the idea for the film when she went to see a slide-show presentation by Puerto Rican, Anna Nieto-Gómez at The Inner City Cultural Center in Los Angeles. Both Morales and Nieto-Gómez were attending UCLA at the time. Nieto-Gómez created the slide-show to encourage working-class Latinas to strike. Nieto-Gómez began the slide-show by giving Chicanas an idea of their history—Chicana history, not European history. For many Chicanas in the audience, including Morales, this was the first time they had heard *their* history, and the first time they discovered that mexicanas and Chicanas had held powerful roles in the past. So Morales approached Nieto-Gómez after the presentation and asked if she could use Nieto-Gomez's research to create a film about the history of Chicanas. As Morales explains:

> I talked to her afterwards and told her I'd love to adapt the information she had presented and make a movie. [...] I wanted her research. I would later add to her research with my own. She was excited that I [wanted] to make a movie on something she had worked on. She had a friend of hers, Cindy Honesto, who had helped her with her slide show assist me in the research I would be gathering. Cindy was a great help. Cindy had apparently shot a lot of those slides for Anna. So Anna asked Cindy to help me with locate photos Cindy had shot from books. I re-shot some of them on film and found others on my own. (Personal Interview 5/13/04)

Cindy Honesto, Carmen Moreno (who scored the film)

and Carmen Zapata (narrator) helped with the making of *Chicana*, yet Morales did the majority of the work. In fact, Morales lacked any sort of budget. She only had $5,000 to work with so she solicited the help of her family members (as Morales explains):

> All those people in [*Chicana*]? The live action stuff—that's my family! My brothers, my sister, mom, who is now 80 years old. I produced it, shot it, I did the sound. It was 1978—I had dropped out of school for about 5 years, and when I came back to get my masters, and I just had one more year to do, everybody was gone that I knew. I didn't know a soul so I didn't ask anybody to help me. [...] I didn't feel comfortable enough asking anybody for help. I almost had a little nervous breakdown—you know, it's really hard to put a movie together with people but by yourself. Good thing it was a small movie. It's actually the only thing I could have done by myself. (Personal Interview 5/13/04)

With *Chicana,* Morales created a photomontage using Mexican murals by artists Diego Rivera, David Alfaro Siqueiros and José Clemente Orozco, as well as rare photos, prints and documentary footage. *Chicana* tells the story of the Chicana from pre-Columbian times to the present including her role in Aztec society, her involvement in the 1810 struggle for Mexican Independence, her participation in the US Labor Strikes in 1872, her contributions to the 1910 Mexican Revolution and her leadership in recent civil rights struggles. Rashkin notes that "[w]hat is immediately striking about *Chicana* is its attempt to break from [a] pervasive active/passive opposition and using existent male-authored texts, to put fourth a different vision of female agency" (104).

By piecing together pre-existing texts and hence

offering new meanings, *Chicana* shows the important contributions women have made in history as mothers, educators, leaders, workers and activists in spite of their oppressed status. "The movie depicts the oppression that Mexican women endured and celebrates those women who struggled for the vote, education, property rights and for the rights of men as well" (Morales, Personal Interview). *Chicana* offers "...a panoramic view of the development of women's roles" (C. Tatum *Chicano Popular Culture* 86). Therefore, it comes as no surprise that the "film is a tribute to all courageous and freedom loving women in the history of the Mexican Chicano people" (Video). In fact, the film goes against the typical patriarchal plot that renders women invisible, especially Chicana women.

Two scholars, Rosa Linda Fregoso (1993, 1990-1991) and Chon Noriega (1992) claim that *Chicana* imitates Luis Valdez's Teatro Campesino's *I am Joaquín* (1969). Like *I am Joaquín*, *Chicana* uses a photomontage in order to represent history. Clearly though, *Chicana* focuses on the history of Chicanas beginning with the Aztecs. Interestingly enough,

> The two films use the same murals to tell the story of the Conquest, but whereas *Chicana* excerpts from the murals in order to revise their interpretations, *Joaquín* preserves the values of the original paintings. Thus, there are fewer close-ups in the 1969 film, and more pans across large sections of murals. (Rashkin 106)

It is no wonder why Chicanas go back to the Aztecs to tell their story as Ramón Gutiérrez conveys:

> A chronology for Chicana history that began in 1519—not 1848—was not an arbitrary act. Rather, it placed the issues of gender and power at the very center of the political debate about

the future and the past. By choosing 1519, women focused attention on one of Mexico's most famous woman, Doña Marina. (592)

Doña Marina or La Malinche is discussed more extensively later in this chapter (and later ones too), yet it is important to recognize that *Chicana* does represent a history that began in 1519 rather than 1848. La Malinche represents an important symbol to the Chicana Movement—her tarnished legacy and the move to reappropriate her image. In fact, *Chicana's* re-vision of the male-authored texts makes it a female-centered film, whereas its counterpart, *I am Joaquín*, maintaining the standards of the original murals, is male-centered. Whether *Chicana* is an imitation of *I am Joaquín* or not, it, in itself, is innovative for it portrays a side of history ignored in history texts. With this in mind, Chon Noriega makes an interesting point:

In a visual pun on the still photographs [...], Sylvia Morales inserts brief live action shots of women at work in the home, bringing movement—the Movement—into the domestic sphere. In effect, these brief scenes and the persuasive narration privilege the quotidian, and mark it as an arena for the affirmation and resistance of the other social protests. In documenting the female presence within the nationalist paradigm, *Chicana* is an initial step in the representation of a Chicano identity that affirms rather than "transcends" the gender, class, and political divisions within the community." ("Between a Weapon..." 157)

In fact, *Chicana* affirms Chicana cultural nationalism. Debuting in 1979, during the heart of the Chicana Feminist Movement[12358], *Chicana* addresses gender, class and racial stereotypes. It offers a new view of the myths that have been taught in school (Fregoso *The Bronze Screen* 2). By doing so, *Chicana* takes it one step further by criticizing dominant as well as Chicano oppressive ideals, therefore offering a "counterdiscourse to dominant ideology" (Fregoso *The Bronze Screen* 3). Morales knows the comparison has been made between *Chicana* and *I am Joaquín*:

> I know—they're seen as book ends. They've been compared and contrasted. The comparison mostly, I believe is that we both used the art of Mexican masters to tell our stories. I believe for both of us it was a matter of no budget. Also we're celebrating our culture. The contrast is *Joaquín* excluded women and *Chicana* included men. However, I didn't consciously make *Chicana* as a response to *Joaquín*. I made it because the historical aspects that Nieto-Gómez presented moved me. It motivated me to get the word out about our history. (Personal Interview 5/13/04)

So, yes, in many ways *Chicana* closely resembled *I am Joaquín* as it has been pointed out by Rosa Linda Fregoso and Chon Noriega, however, as Morales states, her intentions were different than that of Valdez—although *Chicana* might have been a response, *Chicana* certainly was not intentional on Morales' part.

One counterdiscourse is the revision of the myth of La Malinche. *Chicana*, like many works by Chicanas of its time, offers a retelling of the myth of La Malinche. As Rashkin points out, the values associated with La Malinche and *La Virgen de Guadalupe* both underwent revision:

> The values [. . .] persisted within a Mexican/Chicano culture that was neither homogenous in its thinking nor unified around the church, so that when Chicana feminists chose to address these

two female figures in their own work, they were responding both to the traditional beliefs that shaped their upbringing *and* to the cultural movements and texts that constituted their heritage as artists and intellectuals. (104)

Many scholars have noted the importance of these archetypes to Chicanas, especially that of La Malinche. Historically, La Malinche/Malintzín/Doña Marina was the Náhuatl woman (rather, the child) who was a mere 14 years old when she was sold as a slave to Hernán Cortés, the Spanish conqueror, when he arrived in Mexico. Because of her linguistic abilities (she spoke Maya, Náhuatl and Spanish); she became a translator for Cortés. Later on, she became Cortés' lover and had his baby (this son would later go to Spain to be educated, and Malinche would marry a soldier of Cortés). Today La Malinche is infamously remembered for the help she gave Cortés that led to his conquest of the Aztec empire.

However, the story of La Malinche has been distorted and abused. "[La Malinche] has been blamed as the ultimate traitor to Mexico and she has also been used to symbolize the total negative essence of the Mexican woman" (García *Chicana Feminist Thought* 116). Furthermore, she represents feminine betrayal within the Chicano community and "has acted as a principal reference point for the masculinist cultural production of Chicano shame" (Gutiérrez-Jones 109-110).

In order to rehabilitate and demystify the relation of La Malinche with the concepts of betrayal and shame, Chicana artists have reinvented La Malinche's archetypal status. Núñez-Noriega says Chicanas have portrayed La Malinche "como mujer inteligente, traicionada por su pueblo, esclavizada por su sexo, admirada por su buen desempeño intelectual, salvadora de la extinción de su pueblo" ("Between a Weapon..." 62).

Taffola states, "[t]he image of La Malinche, throughout Mexican history, has been used against women, until even her name is used as a common synonym to the word "traitor" (16). Furthermore, as Alma M. García goes on to say:

> In their struggle to overcome the particular problems faced by Mexican-American women, Chicana feminists sought encouragement and inspiration from a history and tradition of strong women in their culture including that of the Pre-Columbian past. Revising history and mythology to suit contemporary ideological needs, Chicana feminists such as Adelaida R. Del Castillo proposed that Chicanas identify with historical figures such as Doña Marina (La Malinche) the native princess who assisted Hernán Cortés in his conquest of the Aztec Empire. Rather than the traitor that she is portrayed as in Mexican history, Doña Marina should now be appropriated or resignified as an assertive and independent female figure who herself was struggling against Aztec tyranny. (*Chicana Feminist Thought* 108)

In *Chicana*, La Malinche is referred to by her Aztec name, Malintzín Tenepal. While showing various images, the narration reads:

> In 1519 Spanish conquistadores land in Mexico in search for gold and silver. They find a people revolting against the slavery and tyranny imposed by the Aztec priests. Many of the oppressed Indians unite with the Spaniards in hopes of gaining their freedom. The Tlaxcala nation offers twelve virgin slaves as token of this alliance. One of the slaves Malintzín Tenepal acts boldly to gain her

freedom and becomes an interpreter between Mexican tribes and the Spaniard. The Spaniards call her "Doña Marina," the Indians, "La Malinche," but she becomes a symbol of a ravaged Mexico, for the overthrow of the Aztec rulers does not bring freedom. (Video)

By telling the story of La Malinche, *Chicana* takes issue with the myths that have been passed down thought the centuries. Morales explains her re-vision of the Malinche myth:

> I was fascinated by her story and there are variations to the story but either story you go by —she got a raw deal. Malinche was a child when she was sold into slavery [. . .]—which means being a female slave, she was probably raped. [. . .] She's so brilliant she already knows a few languages, that's the main reason she was a good trade for the Spanish or Cortés, and she becomes Cortés' concubine and translator. [. . .] So the story goes that she was called "La Malinche" [it means traitor] by the Mexican Indians or Aztecs. [. . .] She's also known as "la Chingada," which literally means, "the fucked one" [. . .] And here she is, a slave, first to some tribe and then to the Spanish. What choices does she have? This teenager is accused of selling out Mexico. How is this possible? Somebody that was powerless, who was a slave? It's a fascinating story. It's an important story in the history of Mexico because her child, she had a baby by a Spaniard, is considered the first Mestizo and she's considered the Benedict Arnold of Mexico. I haven't kept up with the most current philosophical thinking in Mexico, so I don't know if this legend still holds as it did when *Chicana* was made. I do know that

she will always be some kind of legend, positive or negative. (Personal Interview 5/13/04)

Rosa Linda Fregoso elaborated on this topic—offering an analysis of the Malinche myth in her book, *The Bronze Screen*:
> This view of woman as treacherous informs the imagination of such Mexican writers as Octavio Paz and Carlos Fuentes, who have traced the pathology of Mexicans (mestizos) to La Malinche's rape by the conqueror. In their view, La Malinche facilitates the ultimate downfall, giving birth to the mestizo people. [...] Hence, she is called *la chingada* ("the fucked one"), and her descendants, the Mexican people, *los hijos de la chingada* ("children of the fucked one"). [...] Chicana intellectuals, scholars as well as creative artists, have reconfigured the Malintzín myth by drawing upon historical accounts of the conquest that disclose the extent of her oppression in pre-Columbian Mexico. (16-17)

Like fellow Chicana intellectuals and scholars, Morales delivers an objective re-presentation of the Malinche myth in the film, alluding to the recognition of Malinche as a strong and important woman of Chican@ history. In fact, *Chicana* focuses on her role as a translator and advisor, rather than the portrayal of her as a traitor or sell-out. Rashkin points out that Chicana feminists' revision of La Malinche breaks the silence:
> While Malintzín's act of translation proved most dangerous to herself, ending ironically in her own silence, modern feminists utilize tactics of translation and revision to question the fate of Malintzín, and that of all women who have

been silenced, in order to move towards a more positive future. (117)

Malinche is not the only woman that regains her voice through the film. It also mentions other celebrated women of Chicana history.

In order to bring a name and recognition to other important women in Chicana history, *Chicana* commemorates women like Sor Juana Inés de La Cruz, Lucy Gonzáles Parsons, Emma Tenayuca, Dolores Huerta, Alicia Escalante and Francisca Flores—bringing to light the lineage of strong Chicana women in order to empower Chicanas today. Hence, *Chicana* battles the old myths, bringing to life Chicana reality and bringing Chicanas out of the oppression they have been under by raising consciousness and revising history so that it was not the classical one-dimensional history that is so often portrayed. The ultimate goal for Morales "was to let people know what Chicanas/Mexicanas had contributed historically to the culture and to put out a feminist take on that history" (Phone Interview with Sylvia Morales, 5/14/04). This is clearly stated in the film by the narrator, Carmen Zapata, of the film:

> Where does this kind of learning come from? This is not really taught in the schools. And unless one specialized in the history of the Chicana may one ever really become aware of their background and heritage as a woman? This kind of project is necessary to make Hispanic woman realize her value and worth by becoming aware of her roots. (Morales "*Filming a Chicana*" 311)

To know one's history gives one a sense of self, a sense of who one is. Not only does *Chicana* finally bring light to Chicana history for Chicanas, but also it enlightens Chicanos and others of the dominant group that have been denied such an education. Because of *Chicana*, the richness of heritage of the Chicana, and the contributions she has made to culture and society will no longer be ignored, for the film gives Chicanas a rightful voice, an image and a name that were overdue.

Chapter 6
Puppet: A Novella (1985)

The Chicana writer, by the fact that she is
  even writing in today's society,
is making a revolutionary act. Embodied in the
  act of writing is her voice
against others' definitions of who she is
  and what she should be.
There is, in her open expression and in the
  very nature of opening up,
a refusal to submit to a quality of silence
that has been imposed upon her for
  centuries.
—Rita Sánchez

In her article, "*The Development of Chicana Feminist Discourse 1970-1980,*" Alma M. García expresses how Chicana feminist discourse emerged in the 1970s through the 1980s:

> The years between 1970 and 1980 represented a formative period in the development of Chicana feminist thought in the United States. During this period, Chicana feminists addressed the specific issues affecting Chicanas as women of color in the United States. As a result of their collective efforts in struggling against racial, class, and gender oppression, Chicana feminists developed an ideological discourse that addresses three major issues. These were the relationship between Chicana feminism and the ideology of cultural nationalism, feminist baiting within the Chicano movement, and the

relationship between the Chicana feminist movement and the white feminist movement. (217)

While García's article only covers 1970-1980, the fight against gender oppression has not ceased to exist. Many of the struggles still exist today, and that is why we see the fight for justice in new books. In the books that arose as a result of the Chicana Feminist Movement, Chicanas combated two forms of their oppression, namely, race (how they were linguistically oppressed from Spanish but also how they have been ethnically oppressed) and gender (how they were sexually oppressed).

To combat gender oppression, Chicanas began to contextualize their sexuality, as a method of liberation and as a way to give themselves their own voice and identity. In the introduction of the anthology, *The Sexuality of Latinas*, editors Norma Alarcón, Ana Castillo and Cherríe Moraga address the repression of the sexuality of Chicanas in society:

> Our sexuality has been hidden, subverted, distorted within the "sacred" walls of the *"familia"*—be it myth or reality—and within the even more privatized walls of our bedrooms. Like many women, our understanding of our sexual desire too often comes through the reality of sexual violence. In the journey to the love of the female self and each other we are ultimately forced to confront father, brother, and god (and mother as his agent). (9)

As a result, many Chicana writers have included sexual episodes with sexual references in their novels/writings. As Chabram-Dernersesian observes ". . .contemporary Chicana writers and poets have opened up the gate to human sexuality, giving Chicana subjects back their desire (both heterosexual and gay)" (93). By confronting the subject of female sexuality, Chicanas liberate themselves from the taboos of society. As far as "sexuality" is concerned in this chapter and those that follow, the norm is that the heterosexuality of a woman is addressed. Sexuality is reduced to the quality or the state of being sexual, the condition of having sex, the activity of sex and/or the expression of sexual desires. The expression of sexuality in Chicana narrative tends to shock the reader. Margarita Cota-Cárdenas points out that she expresses sexuality because "[W]e are all sexual beings, so why not rejoice in it?" (Personal Interview 5/16/04). This expression of sexuality is a form of rebellion against the norms of Chicana and Angla society—as a way to break from patriarchal control. Gonzáles-Berry confesses, "the writing of the Chicana Body flies in the face of patriarchy" ("Re: *Paletitas de Guayaba.*" 1). To write and express sexuality is a way to demystify masculine power.

However, sexuality is not the only oppression these Chicana writers address in their novellas. Another is linguistic oppression. As a way to deflate prejudice attitudes toward bilingualism, Chicana writers began acknowledging their roots through language. Chicanas began to write in Spanish or a mixture of Spanish and English to show their true cultural identity. As Anzaldúa has been quoted for years, "[e]thnic identity is twin skin to linguistic identity, I am my language" (59). Therefore, it comes as no surprise that many Chicana writers use language to identify with their "ethnic" identity. Certainly, oppression of language is considered racial oppression because bilingualism (sometimes speaking three languages is a part of the Chicana race) is a part of one's ethnicity, one's race. Of course, Spanish is an important part of the Chican@ because of his/her history in North America. As known, Chicanas are of Mexican origin—they, their parents, grandparents and/or great-grandparents are originally from Mexico. Therefore, their language is not only the English they acquired in the United States, but also the Spanish that is spoken in the home or by their ancestors. It comes as no surprise that Chicanas address this very issue in their writings.

Through the artistic works that Chicanas created, Chicanas were on a journey of discovery. Tey Diana Rebolledo points this out in the introduction to *Puppet*:

> These journeys have been searches toward understanding what it means to be a woman, *Mexicana*, Chicana, *Americana*, in male dominated societies. These writers slip between two distinct cultures in order to create a fluid third space, and they challenge the norms of both Anglo and Hispano cultures. The novels of these writers [Denise Chávez, Helena María Viramontes, Sandra Cisneros, Pat Mora, Erlinda Gonzáles-Berry, and Margarita Cota-Cárdenas] are distinctly original works that explore politics, culture, social life, and self-representations of Chicanas in the Unites States. (xvi)

Specifically, Chicanas combat their race and gender oppression through literature. One of the first Chicanas to address this was, Margarita Cota-Cárdenas in her novel, *Puppet: una novella chicana*. Cota-Cárdenas initiates her response in the subtitle of the book: "I wanted to emphasize the nature of the subject: about Chican@ reality, a short novella, and a possible play on the combination of "nov-ella" (a new novel by a 'she')" (Personal Interview 5/16/04).

In fact while addressing race and gender oppression, Chicana literature "...touches virtually every aspect of the Chicana experience with remarkable sympathy, intensity, acuity, and realism" (Mirandé and Enríquez 179). As

Chicana feminist scholar Yvonne Yarbro-Bejarano explains, by writing:
> the Chicana writer finds that the self she seeks to define and love is not merely an individual self, but a collective one. In other words, the power, the permission, the authority to tell stories about herself and other Chicanas comes from her cultural, racial/ethnic and linguistic community. (215)

We see this in *Puppet* by Margarita Cota-Cárdenas. Published originally in 1985, *Puppet*, tells the story of Petra Leyva and how she understands the assassination of Puppet, a Chicano youth, and the subsequent police cover-up. Clearly, through the multiple-voice narrative, Cota-Cárdenas questions the codes of conduct of the Mexican/Chicano patriarchal culture (Shuru 9). As Villarreal adds, "*La narrativa de Cota-Cárdenas es una expiación de múltiples asuntos sociales y políticos, de las chicanas que se atreven a criticar las tradiciones machistas y las limitaciones de la cultura chicana*" (27). After all, in reference to the Chicana Feminist Movement "...the Chicana had to give herself her own value and definition, avoiding the trendy overtures of the men and mainstream feminists, both of whom only promised to deliver a life in the service of others" (Chabrám-Dernersesian 86-87). In *Puppet*, Cota-Cárdenas reflects on tradition while at the same time she questions the rules of society. Charles Tatum reiterates this idea when he comments on Cota-Cárdenas writing: "*Margarita Cota-Cárdenas afirma su independencia y establece su identidad como chicana por medio del erotismo. [...] [Rechaza] la vergüenza tradicionalmente* asociada con el placer sexual" (*La literatura chicana* 231).

In *Puppet*, Cota-Cárdenas uses Petra's feminine voice[12359] (for the most part) in order to convey sexual episodes and various intimate perspectives of sexuality. Cota-Cárdenas stated that there are two passages that relate directly to sexuality in the novel: "the "Vittorio *entra en su apartamento*" passage, and the "Discurso de la Malinche" passage" (Personal e-mail 11/19/02). First, the passage "Vittorio *entra en su apartamento*" (Vittorio enters his apartment) recounts the fantasy that Petra has with her ex-husband[12360]:

...*Ha sido un día largo, demasiado largo y ahora ustedes dos, quieren ser ustedes dos, y se van abrazados cuando surge de la nada una orquestra a todo dar, y se van bailando un vals de Vienna...por casualidad—Vittorio es muy, pero muy sofisticado—llegan a la recámara, al lado de la cama, y sin ningún esfuerzo aparente, se te cae el pegnoir del negligée...—Vittorrio te susurra:—C'est vraiment un soirée, n'est ce pas? Y tú, Petrina casada y feliz para siempre, le contestas, levemente jadeante,—Oh, pero OUI OUI my pet! Y entonces ustedes dos...*

BBRRRIIIIIIINNNNGGGGG

No, todavía no te hace ring el bell, todavía no...Ustedes dos no quieren contestar el teléfono, porque en ese momento le desabrochas los pantalones rosita y rete apretados a Vittorio tu marido y le salta—PLINNG! el pene ancho, largo, oscuro y pulsante, y tú lo coges en la mano suave pero fuertemente, sí es posible, y la murmuras al oído mientras mientras lo empujas a la cama y brincas sobre él, el pene digo, y rechinando rechinando le gritas bajito, sí es posible,—Oh, oh pero OUI sí sí uy uy uy mi pirulí...! (43-45)

Neither one of you want to answer the telephone because you just can't wait anymore...It has been a long day, too long and now you want it to be just the two of you, and you're walking arm in arm when out of nowhere an orchestra explodes into song to which you dance a Vienna waltz...and by chance—Vittorio is very, very sophisticated—you arrive to the bedroom, next to the bed, and without any apparent effort, your pegnoir del negligée falls to the floor...Vittorio whispers: "C'est vraiment un soirée, n'est ce pas?" And you forever happy married Petrina, answer him breathy voice, "Oh, pero OUI OUi my pet!" and then the two of you...

BBRRRIIIIIIINNNNGGGGG

No, he doesn't make your bell ring, not yet...Neither of you want to answer the phone because at this moment you're unzipping Vittorio, your husband's, very tight rose-colored pants and then—PLINNG! His wide, long, dark, pulsating penis jumps out and you take it softly but strongly in your hand, yes it is possible, and you murmur in his ear as you push him onto the bed and jump on top of it, the penis I mean, squealing squealing you softly yell, yes, it's possible, "Oh, oh pero OUI yes yes uy uy uy mi pirulí ...!" (47-48)

Here, Petra "was laughing at herself for being so

romantic at this time of emotional crisis (whether to get involved in Puppet's incident and story or not)" (Personal e-mail 11/19/02). This is evident because Petra calls herself "*romanticaca*". While Petra had this great fantasy with Vittorio, she describes to Memo on the phone[12361] (45) that they were only "*haciendo tortillas.*" Of course, here Cota-Cárdenas makes light of Petra's fantasy, but also she equates the act of making love to making tortillas[12362]. This fantasy and sexual experience is part of Petra's personal growth and her liberation as a Chicana in the novel. Moreover, as Xochitl Estrada Shuru notes of Cota-Cárdenas in *Puppet* in her dissertation, *The Poetics of Hysteria in Chicana Writing: Sandra Cisneros, Margarita Cota-Cárdenas, Pat Mora, and Bernice Zamora*, "...Cota-Cárdenas and other Chicanas strongly speak of the failure of the Chicano Movement to integrate within its political agenda issues of gender equality" (179). Therefore, Cota-Cárdenas takes advantage of an opportunity like *Puppet* to include sexual references, or better yet, sexual fantasies like, "Vittorio entra en su apartamento", in order to address issues of gender equality in the Chicano community.

Cota-Cárdenas continues to debate these issues in "Malinche's discourse"[12363] that also occupies an entire chapter in the novel (87-98) and that co-editors Rebolledo and Rivero include in their book, *Infinite Divisions*, as an example of how Chicana writers address myths and archetypes (203-207). La Malinche[12364] is an archetype that Chicanas have begun to reinvent through new stories about her. In fact as Alma M. García states:

> In their struggle to overcome the particular problems faced by Mexican-American women, Chicana feminists sought encouragement and inspiration from a history and tradition of strong women in their culture including that of the Pre-Columbian past. Revising history and mythology

to suit contemporary ideological needs, Chicana feminists such as Adelaida R. Del Castillo proposed that Chicanas identify with historical figures such as Doña Marina (La Malinche) the native princess who assisted Hernán Cortés in his conquest of the Aztec Empire. Rather than the traitor that she is portrayed as in Mexican history, Dona Marina should now be appropriated or resignified as an assertive and independent female figure who herself was struggling against Aztec tyranny. (*Chicana Feminist Thought* 108)

Therefore, it is no surprise that Cota-Cárdenas does so in *Puppet*$_{12365}$:

¿Éres tú Malinche malinchi? ¿Quién eres tú (¿Quién soy YO malinchi?)/vendedor o comprador? ¿Vendido o comprado y a qué precio? ¿Qué es ser lo que tantos gritan dicen vendido-a malinchi-e qué es qué son/somos qué? a qué precio sin haber estado allí nombrar poner labels etiquetas qué quiénes han comprado vendido malinchismo qué otros —ismos inventados gritados con odio reaccionando saltando como víboras como víboras SUS OJOS como víboras qué quién qué

[...]

—Usando la terminología tan de moda y tan útil hoy día, les voy a contar de mis años formativos: a la edad de cinco, más o menos, dejé de ser la hija mayor predilecta de mi tribu, cuando me vendieron algunos parientes muy próximos, a unos compadres más lejanos, que me compraron...a qué precio? (87-88)

Are you Malinche a malinchi? Who are you (who am I malinchi)? seller or buyer? sold or bought and at what price? What is it to be what

> so many shout say sold-out malinchi who is who are/are we what? at what price without having been there naming putting labels tags what who have bought sold malinchismo what other –ismos invented shouted with hate reacting striking like vipers like snakes THEIR EYES like snakes what who what
> [...]
> "Using the latest terminology and it's so useful nowadays, I'm going to tell you about my formative years: at the age of five, more or less, I left off being the favorite eldest daughter of my tribe, when some very immediate relatives sold me, to some more distant buddies, who bought me...at what price? (93-94).

As illustrated in this quote from the text, Cota-Cárdenas first attacks Chicano culture for perpetuating the myth of La Malinche. Cota-Cárdenas explains that "Malinche's Discourse" in the novella is "another example of my 'anti-myths and counter-legends' *onda*" (Personal Interview 5/16/04). Cota-Cárdenas accentuates the fact that La Malinche was sold and bought as an object (this is evident by the use of bold letters). She puts emphasis on the fact that it is "so useful" to know the truth about La Malinche today. Falsified history tells us that the word "Malinche" signifies a woman who has been a traitor to her country or community—*una vendida* (a sell-out). Cota-Cárdenas show us how the history of La Malinche or better yet, the stereotypes that come with the name of La Malinche are part of the history of men. In fact, Malinche's history needs to be revisited and rediscovered to know the truth.

For Chicana writers, La Malinche is the victim and is the conquered—not the sell-out and traitor. In regards to the

La Malinche passage, Cota-Cárdenas explains: "it's an obvious rewriting of the myths, subversion and attack of the Mexican/Latino myths surrounding Malinche and her historical archetype" ("Re: Puppet..." 11/25/02). According to Tey Diana Rebolledo in her introduction in the book *Sanctuaries of the Heart/santuarios Del Corazon: A Novella in English And Spanish* by Cota-Cárdenas, she mentions that in *Puppet*, Cota-Cárdenas:

> subverts the traditional image of Malinche as a traitor [...] representing her as a woman who not only questions traditional values that keep women in place but a woman who achieves her own power by questioning the historical representations of her actions and imposing her own history. (4)

Clearly, Cota-Cárdenas' Malinche is a rewriting of the traditional myth. By rewriting La Malinche, Cota-Cárdenas demystifies the Mexican Latino myths surrounding Malinche and her historical archetype[12366].

Through the experiences of Petra, Cota-Cárdenas takes the opportunity to bring to the reader's attention, the problems of the Chicano Movement, for example, expression of sexuality in the Chicano community. From a feminist view, she discusses a woman's eroticism and the relations between a woman and a man. Additionally, Petra's mental state, that of paranoia, "...serves not only to object to the rigid religious, political and social constructs imposed upon a marginalized gender but also to initiate the emancipation of a neglected Chicano people" (Shuru 161). Like her writings, Petra's sexual (and other) experiences allow her to find her own identity that she has been denied. On the second to last page of the novel Petra knows that, "...hay que seguir adelante con humor con huevos-ovarios con lo único que puedes que eras tú" (138) "you have to go on seguir adelante con valor con humor with balls-ovaries with all you've got" (145). Until the very end, Cota-Cárdenas takes the opportunity to make the woman equal to the man, with the words "balls-ovaries"—equating the sexual organs of a man and a woman respectively$_{12367}$. In this way, Cota-Cárdenas helps to alleviate the weight of oppression through the inclusion of the sexuality.

Cota-Cárdenas uses Petra's daughter, María, to also talk about the Chicano Movement in the novella. María is in college in the novella and calls home to speak with her mother. María, surrounded by and emerged in all the activism at her college campus, is very interested in her bicultural reality as well as in the Chicano Movement, Cesar Chávez, the March of Delano, etc. Cota-Cárdenas explains that she purposely included María's character to discuss and bring up the Chicano Movement:

[María] is the prototype of the young Chicana student-activist, a foil to pique Petra's indecision to continue forward with the investigation of Puppet's death, writing about it, make a personal, social and political commitment, etc. It also reminds Petra about her own dark secret: she had not supported the March in 1965. I had a similar experience, but have been a long-time supporter of the United Farm Workers. In fact, that same campus developed one of the first Chicano Studies Programs in California in the late 60s; I was one of the members of that committee. [...] You just do your part to help in the struggle for peace, love, justice, and that's what María in *Puppet* represents. (Personal Interview 5/16/04)

Like Petra, many Chican@s because they were mainly working-class people did not have the opportunity to participate in many of the activities of the Chicano Movement. Petra was occupied by Puppet's murder, but her daughter, María, still represented the struggle for love, justice and peace. In addition to looking at racial oppression through characters like María and her involvement/interest in the Chicano Movement, *Puppet* also addresses linguistic oppression: Cota-Cárdenas wrote *Puppet* in Spanish initially. It was not until the bilingual version was published in 2000 that she translated it into English.[12368] Although it is "translated" there are still key phrases in the English version that are not translated from Spanish—simply because they would not make any sense. Tey Diana Rebolledo has pointed out in her book, *Women Singing in the Snow* that choosing to write in Spanish has its problems:

...it is not a simple question for writers in Spanish to choose this language. It is, in fact, a political act and a declaration of loyalties. It is, particularly from Cota-Cárdenas and Gonzáles-Berry, an act of resistance, and one that leads to a separation from mainstream readers and makes it difficult for them to have their work reviewed and published. (172)

Cota-Cárdenas decided to take the road less traveled by writing in Spanish. As Cota-Cárdenas conveys:

My creative writing seemed to blossom in Spanish. My first poems in the early and mid 70s were almost entirely in Spanish. Then Puppet's core story in 1975 was in English because I had tried to get it published in the (English) newspaper, I was so outraged at what had happened, just like Petra Leyva expresses it in the novel only she (the principal narrator) voices the rage, frustration, etc. mostly in Spanish with some English. That's how I thought about it, and the Ideal reader of the story would be a Spanish-speaking, perhaps bilingual reader who wanted to know what living in the Southwest USA as a Chicano/Chicana might be like. Hopes, fears, joys, funny and sad, scary—most of it I wanted to say it as I was feeling it—in my secret heart's language, Spanish/from a woman born in the USA, but whose first language had been New Mexican/Mexican/borderlands Spanish. ("Re: more puppet…" 4/22/03)

By writing in Spanish, she was able to identify more closely with her heritage and cultural roots and resist societal oppression.

In conclusion, Margarita Cota-Cárdenas' *Puppet* is a perfect example of Chicanisma. It gives Chicanas a voice, specifically, a bilingual one. It gives Chicanas an image, a sexually free one, and it gives Chicanas a name, one without the connotations of La Malinche. Written in Spanish and later published in English and Spanish, openly expressing sexual episodes and desires and by retelling the myth of La Malinche, *Puppet* demystifies masculine as well as Anglo power.

Chapter 7
La Ofrenda: The Days of the Dead (1988)

> The word death is not pronounced
> in New York, Paris or London,
> because it burns the lips.
> The Mexican in contrast, is familiar
> with death,
> jokes about it, caresses it, sleeps with
> it, celebrates it,
> it is one of his favorite toys and
> most steadfast love.
> —Octavio Paz (quoted from *La Ofrenda*)

A decade after the appearance of *Chicana* and a mere three years after *Puppet*, *La Ofrenda: The Days of the Dead* (1988) was made. A film by Lourdes Portillo and Susana Blaustein Muñoz, *La Ofrenda* explores the Mexican and Chican@ celebration of The Days of the Dead, which occurs every year on the first and second days of November. *La Ofrenda* "explores the pre-Hispanic roots of this religious celebration [The Days of the Dead] and the social dimensions of death" (Charles Tatum *Chicano Popular Culture* 87).

Argentinean born and raised, Latino-Jewish identified, Muñoz made the film as a tribute to her father who died very young, and Portillo's goal was to explore her cultural heritage. As noted by Fregoso, "it was not until [*La Ofrenda*] that Portillo decided to make a film about the Chican@ experience" (*Lourdes Portillo* 2). The two filmmakers, after their success with *Las Madres: The*

Mothers of Plaza de Mayo[12369]—the film was nominated for an Academy Award for Best Documentary—PBS provided them with funding to complete *La Ofrenda*. Muñoz, who looks for social justice in her films, decided to deal with the Chicano relationship to the dominant culture in the film. Her ultimate goal was to share a bi-cultural experience with the audience. Portillo, Mexican born and Chicana identified, has focused on the search for Latino identity in her films. Juan Velasco points out that:

> Lourdes Portillo is one of the few Chicanas who, during the last 14 years, has written and directed films while expanding the documentary format [...] An insightful portrayal of the complex experiences shaped by border identities, the Chicana experience emerges in her films as transgression of the cultural hegemonic forces on both sides of the border and as an interruption of the homogeneity and territoriality in both Mexico and the United States. In fact, the crossing of cultures and languages becomes one of the most important characteristics of her work. In her films, Portillo creates a new visual language, with a blend of documentary and poetic self-awareness, switching between cultures in order to map a space in which the audience can see the many voices of the Chicana experience. (245)

Raised in both Mexican and American cultures, Portillo is able to give voice and identity to herself and many others in similar situations through her films. Documentary allows Portillo to revisit her cultural heritage, while at the same time attempting to explain the Mexican and Chican@ culture to the foreign (US-Anglo) culture (Kotz 66). As a feminist, Portillo has also

commented:
> In creating a film one has to internalize authority in order to assert it, and in our culture the assertion of authority by women is not looked upon kindly. It represents the denial of all of our upbringing as women: we are taught to acquiesce, to mediate, to console, to serve and never to demand, because to demand is seen as a masculine quality. (280)

Through recognition of her oppression as a Chicana woman, Portillo has been able to create innovative and empowering films.

La Ofrenda does not fall short of these parameters. As a multi-faceted film, it can be explored and interpreted in many ways. The three crucial themes presented in the film are those of the Mexican/Chican@ celebration of The Days of the Dead, the affirmation of bi-cultural reality of the Chican@ people and the resistance to the acceptance of homosexuality in Mexican culture.

Primarily, as the film's title suggests, *La Ofrenda* addresses the Days of the Dead. Through the form of documentary, Portillo and Muñoz explore this Mexican tradition in which the dead are celebrated and honored. On these days, the dead are greeted with affection and respect as people parade through the streets to the cemetery bearing gifts. Homemade altars are erected with food, candles, flowers and photos of those who have passed into the next world.

Eventually, the film moves from a Mexican village to San Francisco, California tracing the migration of this unique tradition. The transition of the film to San Francisco is crucial to understanding the link the film is drawing between Mexican and Chican@ communities. By celebrating The Day of the Dead, the Chican@ is reminded of her/his ancestral past, and s/he acknowledges that s/he shares a common ancestor with her/his relatives south of the border. The adaptation of this holiday by Chican@s incorporates only one day in November. While only one day in the Chican@ community, the celebration still holds the concept of life through death and assists in capturing the intensity of Mexican culture. In the course of the exploration of this holiday, the film looks into a non-traditional view of attitudes towards death and the dead. This idea is reinforced when several white American tourists visiting Mexico during the celebration are interviewed.

Portillo mentions that they had no plans of including the tourists when the original script was drawn:

> Well, it was just interesting how there was this difference in understanding of death—it was like a clash of cultures. You know you're looking at life and death this way, and this ancient culture is looking at this other way—I think that now perhaps there could be a bridge between those two. I think there is more of an understanding of Mexican culture now. It was just fortuitous that those people [the white tourists] were there at that point. And I asked them, and that's what they came up with. (Personal Interview 5/10/04)

Such a fortuitous encounter offered the perfect juxtaposition between Chican@/mexican@ culture and U.S. Anglo culture. As Kathleen Newman mentions in her article, "Steadfast Love and Subversive Acts: The Politics of *La Ofrenda: The Days of the Dead:*" "The responses of the tourists are striking for what they reveal about anglo xenophobia and ignorance [...] Every answer reveals a complete inability to conceptualize history and culture, let alone another culture's concept of death" (295). The film, therefore, offers a unique look into the Mexican perspective of death, one that stands out against the narrow view of European-American traditions. Newman's quote also alludes to *La Ofrenda*'s second theme, that is, the Anglo's "complete inability to conceptualize history and culture." The film addresses Anglo's ignorance of Chican@ culture and history. Muñoz mentions that "*La Ofrenda* is an indictment against Anglo culture for its ignorance towards other cultures." (Interview with Muñoz, 5/1/04). Since Lourdes Portillo is Chicana identified, she is aware of her community's situation:

> ...going through a Chicana experience made me aware of the fact that there are certain types of obligation that I have toward my community [...] I am bound to a whole community of people [...] I am indeed channeling a whole peoples' kind of concerns. (Velasco 249)

Portillo is aware that she must affirm Chican@ culture and history within the multicultural United States. Fregoso says how she does this in *La Ofrenda*:

> *La Ofrenda* at one level is about the Day of the Dead celebration, but at a deeper level the film is about Chicana identity, and about how one negotiates that identity when crossing the border back and forth and coming into contact with traditions that cross back and forth. (*Lourdes Portillo* 45)

There is no doubt that Chicana/Mexicana identity is emphasized in the film. The film is narrated in both masculine and feminine voices and as Portillo says, the masculine voice is "more of the cerebral, historical point of view, and the feminine view had to do more with the internal, emotional voice" (Velasco 248). Even the flyer of the film hinted at the fact that the film is a "Chicana's quest to understand her culture" (Newman 286).

Additionally, Portillo says the reason she focuses on *la mujer* is because "...mothers are always the ones that carry the tradition [...] in *La Ofrenda* I wanted to make the point very clear, that it was women who celebrated the Day of the Dead, that it was women who did all the work, and the altars, everything" (Velasco 248). Portillo explains that the film "focuses on women as carriers of cultures . . .women are the ones that retain culture but not in a very conscious way just by making food, serving food, by collecting food. . ." (Personal Interview 5/10/04). By focusing on the Chicana, *La Ofrenda* gives the Chicana back her voice that has been silenced.

Addressing the voice of the Mexicana all the way to the Chicana, the film relates Chican@ culture with Mexican culture, conveying that there is not always a border at times. In fact, *La Ofrenda* focuses more on cultural or racial identity, rather than a national identity. As Gloria Anzaldúa conveys in her book, *Borderlands*:

> We say *nosotros los mexicanos* (by *mexicanos* we do not mean citizens of Mexico; we do not mean a national identity, but a racial one). We distinguish between *mexicanos del otro lado* and *mexicanos de este lado*. Deep in our hearts we believe that being Mexican has nothing to do with which country one lives in. Being Mexican is a state of soul—not one of mind, not one of citizenship. (62)

In *La Ofrenda*, Portillo channels this "state of soul" through common culture. This link is accomplished through the common indigenous past the two communities share—as the feminine narrator[12370] mentions at the beginning of the film, "I'm obsessed with the past with things that were only hinted at in my school text books [...] What is there of my Indian past? I weep at the fall of Tenochitlan" (Video).

Furthermore, the film informs the viewer that before the Spanish, indigenous people used to dedicate an entire month to the celebration of the dead. That is why in the 1970s, the Chican@ art communities revived the tradition of the Day of the Dead because it is a connector of 5,000 to 6,000 years of their indigenous past (Lotz 209). As one Chicana reveals in the film, "Chicanos have revived and adapted *Día de los Muertos*. For them, the past is a never ending source of nostalgia" (Video). *Día de los muertos* is the acknowledgement that Mexicans and Chican@s share the same ancestors and traditions. The film shows that it is important to recover, rediscover, teach and explain cultural traditions.

La Ofrenda recovers, teaches and explains the tradition of The Days of the Dead and within this tradition for Mexicans and Chican@s, death is made to be familiar, ironic and sometimes humorous[12371] (back cover of VHS), unlike in American culture where "death is almost like an obscenity" (*La Ofrenda: The Days of the Dead*). Therefore to combat such opposing opinions (in addition to those of death), Concha Saucedo, a psychologist that has a monologue in the film suggests returning to your roots ("la cultura cura" [culture heals]):

> *Bueno, "la cultura cura"* means it we were to translate literally that "culture heals", and essentially what it means is that there are elements in all cultures that give health to people if they retain those elements' and particularly for Latinos, we have, sometimes we have to separate ourselves from that culture, and that separation, that dislocation has created an imbalance, which in effect is "unhealthy". And when we are saying "*la cultura cura,*" we are saying "return to your culture," maintain your culture, because the

base of your health is there. (*La Ofrenda: The Days of the Dead*)

Perhaps, this is where the biggest connection is drawn. Saucedo mentions that through culture one is able to find the strength one needs; that, no matter where one is or what one is doing, if one goes back to one's roots, one will find the strength to carry on. Newman reinforces this idea: "...by maintaining cultural traditions, Chicanos will heal wounds inflicted by a surrounding anglo culture" (297). This message is being conveyed to Chicanos in the film. No matter the oppression imposed on one from the dominant culture$_{12372}$, one can supersede it through culture.

The third issue, and perhaps the most complicated, is the one that tackles homosexuality (and AIDS). Ironically, the film portrays the Mexican open-minded view of death; while at the same time is "an indictment of the politics of exclusion" (Newman 299) of Mexican acceptance of homosexuality. The masculine narrator in the film states, "In this Day of the Dead celebration, people mock death and gender and whatever else needs a little push" (*La Ofrenda: The Days of the Dead*). Then the feminine narrator says:

> In the rigidity of Mexican society, where rules of behavior have been prescribed for thousands of years, it's in the fiesta and the *comparsa* where we can allow ourselves to be free momentarily, to expose our inner selves to the rest of the community. (*La Ofrenda: The Days of the Dead*)

At this point in the film Newman conveys, "For the first time, the male and female narrators depart from their celebration of their indigenous past and their lament of the horrors of the conquest to critique contemporary Mexican society" (288). All of a sudden it is brought to the screener's attention that the open-mindedness of death in Mexican society does not hold true for gender sexuality in a Mexican patriarchal society. This is evident when "Lourdes Portillo and Susana Muñoz offer their spectators a coded image of a cross-dresser, rendering visually what verbal discourse alone cannot" (Fregoso *The Bronze Screen* 118). This juxtaposition between visual and verbal discourse allows for the understanding of intolerance of homosexuality in Mexican culture.

The transition to San Francisco in the film not only highlights the commonalities and linkages between Chican@s and Mexicans, but also the Latino gay community. By doing so, the film parallels the Mexican religious ritual and the altars made in the United States to honor the deaths caused by AIDS. By making these connections, Portillo [and Muñoz are] making radical claims about the Latino diaspora and the collective identity of Latinos that is ultimately deterritorialized, but remains unified by cultural and religious ritual. (2)

Really the Day of the Dead celebration is the same idea for both Chican@s and Mexicans but in the context of mourning for loved ones who are dying of AIDS and who are the dead because they are not accepted in either society (Mexican and Anglo) and yet, there is a pull towards their roots to use Mexican ritual to help the Chican@ gay community come to terms with death.

La Ofrenda: The Days of the Dead is an innovative, creative work done by Lourdes Portillo and Susana Muñoz to "offer" the flaws not only in Anglo-American society, but also Mexican patriarchal society. Certainly, nativism ideals and the ignorance of other cultures in Anglo-American society are more scrutinized in the film. This is emphasized by the "extensive narration [in the film] to explain the Mexican practices and their history to audiences in the U.S." (Kotz 66). This extensive narration is an attempt to make up for the lack of general knowledge about Mexican historical traditions among Anglo-Americans.

So in an attempt to erase this ignorance and nativism, *La Ofrenda* "...reinforces pride in one's culture among Chicano[s] [...] and deepens the understanding of Chicano and Mexican culture among non-Chicanos" (Newman 287). *La Ofrenda* is an offering to the Chican@ and Mexican communities as an act of love[12373] from the filmmakers. The film not only connects the indigenous backgrounds of both communities[12374], but also by focusing on the dead, the filmmakers were able to draw a connection between all people. The films points out that different cultures have different rituals that also need to be acknowledged. For example, when a matachine artist is interviewed in the film, he says "the way these skeletons look is how we'll all end up looking." Hence, hinting at the fact that, underneath masculine or feminine white, black or brown skin, we are all the same in the end.

It is through the themes of Mexican/Chican@ celebration of The Days of the Dead, the affirmation of bi-cultural reality of the Chican@ people and the resistance to the acceptance of homosexuality in Mexican culture that *La Ofrenda* presents an alternative view and therefore, transmits a new perspective on a voice, image and name for the Chicana.

Chapter 8
Paletitas de Guayaba (1991)

The power of the word and the pleasures of the female body are intimately related.
—Elaine Marks

Like Cota-Cárdenas, Gonzáles-Berry elected to write her novella, *Paletitas de Guayaba*, in Spanish. In fact, whether or not to write her novella in Spanish was something that Gonzáles-Berry discusses in her article "Searching for a Voice: Ambiguities and Possibilities." In the article, Gonzáles-Berry discusses how writing allows for one to remove various layers of oppression that have been built up over the years. While debating to use the colonizer's language or that of her ancestors, Gonzáles-Berry confesses:

> But in the real end, I can only say that when I finally finished peeling back this layer, the first words uttered by my voice were in Spanish. (125)

Yet, as Gonzáles-Berry explains, the Spanish in which she would write would be her multi-dimensional Spanish—from the one she grew up with to the one she used to obtain her Ph.D.:

> ...it was clear to me that my choice of Spanish did not mean that I would limit myself exclusively to a formal code, or *el español culto*, which I had mastered in graduate school. Certainly, this code would provide the foundation, but I had no intention of repressing "peripheral" codes that I knew would surface:

popular forms, particularly those of my native dialect [. . .] caló [. . .] calques [. . .] And, of course, I knew that English [. . .] would not fail to impose itself, reminding Spanish monolingual readers of the "difference"—historical, cultural, linguistic, psychological (*y la lista podría volverse catálogo*)—that marked my text for Chicanidad rather than Mexicanidad." (125)

In reality, all these codes were Gonzáles-Berry's voice as well as other Chicana voices, hence the reason she had to write in them. In fact, as Tey Diana Rebolledo conveys in *Women Singing*:
. . .writing in Spanish is a self-conscious political act that offers another dialectic to the language question; even more so because in addition to the basic Spanish texts in both novels [*Puppet* and *Paletitas de Guayaba*], we have the additionally enriching (and subverting) caló, bilingual, and English language levels. And to add an overlay, we have female-language subjects and thoughts. (172)

Like contextualizing the sexuality of a women, to write in Spanish also goes against the norms of society, making these texts political acts in themselves.

Paletitas de Guayaba, published in 1991, tells the story of a teenager, who travels to and through Mexico. The trip becomes a political and historical journey in which Marina, the protagonist, finds her identity. The journey is a reflection of being Chicana, the consciousness and the cultural conflict of being Chicana are reflected in the novel. When speaking about how she handled narration in the novel, Gonzáles-Berry says:

> I began in the third person, and after several weeks of writing, I stopped. It all sounded so stilted, so unnatural. [...] I finally concluded that if, in fact, I felt insecure about putting my *own* voice on the blank paper, why not let someone else speak for me? I decided to turn the task to narrating over to Mari, the main character in the novella. Thus, hiding behind a mask, believing that it was no longer I who spoke but, rather, a young woman who probably had a great deal in common with myself, I felt free from self-consciousness and from fear of exposure. ("Searching for a Voice" 126)

Gonzáles-Berry uses language in the novel to make various *chispas,* and she uses an ironic tone. Through humorous language and humorous themes, Gonzáles-Berry is able to take the power from the man[12375] and the protagonist, Marina and in so doing, Marina *"acepta y celebra su feminidad, su radical otredad, y la de su pueblo"* (Brakel 129). As far as the amount of humor that was contained in her novel, Gonzáles-Berry states:

> The only thing that I can state with any degree of confidence regarding my use of humor is that I agree with Helene Cixous [...] that it is time for women to turn to humor in order "to replace the tears that culture has caused women to shed," and that through humor I have been able to broach taboo topics, to poke fun at a variety of discourses and, not infrequently, at myself. ("Searching for a Voice" 132)

One episode in which she expresses this is when she compares the act of sneezing to the act of having an orgasm (a taboo subject):

> *Pero sabes que también me gusta cuando no nos*

> *vemos por algún tiempo porque siempre son mucho más intensos mis orgasmos. No sé, duran más. Hoy por ejemplo fue increíble, como una torrente de ola tras ola de espasmos eléctricos. Creí que nunca iba a terminar. ¿Te imaginas lo que sería quedarse uno atascado en un orgasmo perpetuo? Sería algo así como las personas que no pueden dejar de estornudar, placer y agonía. En términos puramente biológicos, el estornudar es semejante al orgasmo, ¿no te parece? A mí, por ejemplo, me encanta estornudar. Siento gran satisfacción y placer al hacerlo.* (Gonzáles-Berry *Paletitas de Guayaba* 63)

Here, Gonzáles-Berry compares the normal act of sneezing to the act of having an orgasm. As Tey Diana Rebolledo points out in *Women Singing*:

> In the linking of the orgasm with the more mundane pleasure of sneezing, Gonzáles-Berry elevates and makes ordinary both experiences: surely it is a uniquely creative female experience that makes the nexus between these two acts. Yet this articulation of female sexuality is also ideology, against the repression and ownership of women. This linguistic articulation of woman's sexuality, the subversion of the masculine myth within the text, are all forms of resistance against erasure and silencing. (178)

Gonzáles-Berry is conscious of linguistic articulation of the sexuality of Marina: it is a form of resistance against the silencing of a man. For this reason, there is a lot of eroticism in the novel. Gonzáles-Berry explains that she is not alone when it comes to addressing sexuality in her writing:

> I think given the Catholic upbringing of many

Chicano writers, taking on sexuality by the horns (to use a very masculine metaphor) was crucial to finding voice. Had we not made sexuality central to our writing, we would still be donning the repressive gag of that patriarchal institution that first introduced us, in the most repressive of ways, to the body. (Personal Interview 4/13/04).

As with any culture, Chican@ culture is inter-related. Catholicism was instilled in many Chican@s, and in many ways, Catholicism had a very repressive nature about it, including sexual repression, especially for women. To be free from this repression, Chicana artists became sexually expressive and so did their characters.

In fact, Marina's sexual journey helps her to find her identity as a woman, and as a Chicana, and as Brakel says, "*por la vía erótica [...] Marina supera su estatus de víctima*" (129). Additionally, the conversations Marina has with Sergio help her to overcome the status of a victim of marginalization:

Sabes que el primero, digo el primer orgasmo, siempre es fantástico, ¿no? Claro, porque es el descargo de una tremenda acumulación de energía, pero de ninguna manera se le acerca ni en intensidad ni en satisfacción al segundo o al tercero. No sé cómo explicarlo, pero estos parecen originar en un sitio mucho más profundo que el primero, especialmente si vienen bien seguiditos. A veces siento que brotan del mero centro de mí ser físico y espiritual. No te rías. No sé cómo más explicarlo. La verdad es que es imposible describir la sensación pero, sans doute, vale la pena, aunque a veces cueste tanto trabajo lograrla. Dime la verdad, ¿no te dan celitos que yo pueda tener un montón de orgasmos sin esperar, digo, sin recuperarme del primero? La otra noche estábamos hablando Toña, Lupe, Isaura y yo, y decidimos que el patriarcado se debe al orgasmo múltiple del género femenino. Estoy hablando en serio. (Gonzáles-Berry *Paletitas de Guayaba* 63-64)

It is the bluntness of Gonzáles-Berry's eroticism that flies in the face of patriarchy. In fact, "to name the unnamable, to speak the unsayable, to articulate clearly without euphemisms the female sexual experience is to find freedom" (Rebolledo *Women Singing* 177). Brakel goes further to say that "*[e]sos impulsos habrán encontrado su represión en la moralidad rural y tradicional de sus padres, en la doctrina católica, y en la confesión—que juntos hacen que ella estalle*" (131). Through confronting eroticism, Marina regains her rights to her body: "*Marina declara haberse deshecho de su bagaje (represivo) cultural. Su cuerpo es suyo. Se deleita en actos sexuales no endosados por la iglesia*" (Núñez-Noriega 65). Moreover, according to Gonzáles-Berry, "To merely TALK about sex is to break a taboo. This is what I was attempting to do in this passage. To express sexual desire is to make public a very private topic" (Personal e-mail 11/21/02). In fact, to speak, to contextualize or to experiment with a sexual act is a way to find freedom, and that's the liberty Gonzáles-Berry finds with *Paletitas de Guayaba*.

Like Cota-Cárdenas, Gonzáles-Berry includes a revision of the masculine myth of La Malinche in her work.[12376] Like Morales, Gonzáles-Berry was fascinated with La Malinche and her treatment by posterity. Gonzáles-Berry explains that the writing of this portion of the book was somewhat of an out-of-body experience, "I can't say I really wrote this section. It simply poured out on the page as if by automatic writing. This was really strange; I felt as if Malinche were really speaking through my pen" (Personal Interview 4/13/04).

The episode with La Malinche in *Paletitas* is one of Marina's dreams (evident by the italics it is in the text). Of course, Gonzáles-Berry includes this passage as an aspect of Marina's metaphorical journey, so that Marina[12377] can find her true identity. As a recommendation to fellow Chicana writers, Gonzáles-Berry mentions the importance of revising myths:

> That we appropriate and revise myths, particularly those that have had as their primary goal the immobilization and the silencing of women. Thus, following the footsteps of [...] Margarita Cota-Cárdenas, and numerous other Mexican and Chicana writers, I created my own revised version of the Malinche Myth. ("Searching for a Voice" 129)

Again, through her writing Gonzáles-Berry takes the opportunity to break the silencing of women. Gonzáles-Berry makes La Malinche the narrator and Malinche is talking to Marina.

Speaking from the past (the time of the Aztecs, more or less), La Malinche offers Marina her vision of what will happen to Tenochtitlan. As well, Malinche warns Marina of the falsified myth that will arrive from Malinche's memory and the sexual oppression men will impose on women in the future:

> *Quiero que comprendas mis acciones para que algún día cuando te hiera la violencia de las palabras, "Hijo de la chingada," entiendas los motivos que me impulsan. Mira las mujeres en esta sociedad, igual que lo serán en la tuya, son meros objetos, son muebles, son la propiedad de sus padres y después de sus esposos. El único honor que se les otorga en esta cultura, es ser sacrificadas, siempre que sean vírgenes. ¡Gran honor!*

> [...] *Las mujeres somos primero los espejos que reflejan la imagen del varón para que se percate de quién es; después somos sus juguetes en el petate y, en fin, receptáculos e incubadoras de sus granos de maíz. Se nos reliega al mundo de la sombra y del silencio; pero ese silencio engendra la palabra que se revuelca en nuestra misma hiel y se vuelve rencor, injuria y también canto; y esta palabra se le agrega otra y otra y terminan en fin siendo una larga y fuerte cadena que nos envuelve y nos estrangula. Podemos rendirnos ante ella, expirar asfixiadas de palabras que nunca encontraron voz, o podemos conjurar, con todos los agüeros del cielo y del infierno, esa voz y volcarla sobre el mundo de los grandes señores.*
> (Gonzáles-Berry *Paletitas de Guayaba* 75-76)

Here, like Cota-Cárdenas, Gonzáles-Berry makes La Malinche into an assertive, independent woman who stands up for herself. Gonzáles-Berry uses La Malinche's voice to talk to the reader and Marina. As Gonzáles-Berry states, in this passage "we hear not the traditional discourse of betrayal ascribed to the mythohistorical figure but, rather, what she might have said about herself as she evaluated history from a female perspective" (129). Gonzáles-Berry revises the masculine myth of La Malinche to set the record straight. She wants to express the subordinate role of women and wants to change it through Malinche's advice. Gonzáles-Berry deviates from the traditional acceptance of this iconic example.[12378] As Martínez points out, "It is through the demystifying of La Malinche that scholars [...] have forced a reconsideration of the "loyalist versus betrayer" binarism, especially as it is tied to Chicanas' sexuality"

(79). With a feminine voice, La Malinche conveys the reality of the sexual oppression in the Chicano community between a man and a woman and offers advice in order to change the situation. La Malinche here represents the importance of independent identity, or better yet, a powerful voice separate from a man's. Through the recognition of and expression of her voice, Gonzáles-Berry creates a narrative that responded to the dominant patriarchal one.

Gonzáles-Berry affirms that her book's purpose is to respond to two dominant narratives, the patriarchal one and the religious one.[2379] She mentions that to give someone a derogatory name (like "La Malinche", "La Llorona" o "*puta*") as institutions like the church or patriarchal society does, is a way to control women.[2380] It is a method of eliminating the independence of a woman and a way of controlling what they want to do with their bodies.[2381] Therefore, in order to liberate themselves from this oppression, Chicana writers write their bodies:

> The ability to write the body and to write sexuality has been instrumental in giving Chicana writers an empowered voice. To become whole, they must be able to seize the voices that articulate the shame, the secrets. Clearly there has been nothing more oppressed than women's sexuality, the lips that cannot speak. (Rebolledo *Women Singing* 183)

Both Cota-Cárdenas and Gonzáles-Berry write and contextualize the body in their works in order to liberate themselves from the oppression of female sexuality.

Writing *Paletitas de Guayaba* was a healing process for Gonzáles-Berry, and as she states, "Uncovering that voice [her voice in the novella], however, had required the peeling away of layer upon later of voice-muffling circumstances" (1999 124). In reality, to free herself from the oppression she had experienced her whole life as a Chicana, Gonzáles-Berry had to strip away painful memories of "voice-muffling circumstances" to find her original true voice. In so doing, she produced a work that not only gave Chicanas a voice as well, but also a name and an image.

Chapter 9
El Espejo/The Mirror (1991)

The bullets are discrete and designed to kill slowly...
These bullets bury deeper than logic.
Racism is not intellectual.
I cannot reason these scars away...
Every day I am deluged with reminders
that this is not
my land—
and this is my land...
—L.D. Cervantes

The third film and fifth work that addresses Chicanisma and that gives voice to the Chicana is *El Espejo/The Mirror* by Frances Salomé España. While not as widely known as *Chicana* or *La Ofrenda*, *El Espejo* is no less creative or innovative. *El Espejo*, a very short film of seven minutes, "...visualizes the thoughts/ images of a young child growing up in the inner city [East L.A.], in a space where the rural and urban intersect: the Chicano barrio" (Fregoso *The Bronze Screen* 120). Perhaps crucial to the understanding of *El Espejo* is its abstract experimental video technique— España uses film and video as an art form. España points out, "The spirit moves. I don't make film/video in traditional ways. I can't afford to, to be honest. I find ways to create, and my process is abstract, but works for me. [...] I don't work with a traditional script. I make notes, write segments, and draw pictures" (Personal Interview 5/16/04). For España, *El Espejo/The Mirror* speaks to her mood, contradictions, memory, dreamtime, her life and experience at the time. With the film, she wanted to re-work or adapt "film language to rasquachi aesthetics and economics" (Personal Interview 5/16/04).

Also vital to the understanding of *El Espejo* is its *testimonio* narrative style. The *testimonio* is given by España who is retelling a dream she once had—literally, España shot it, edited it and did her own acting—she was "all alone in the middle of a room with the camera connected to [her] TV monitor so that [she] could check composition and lighting" (Personal Interview 5/16/04). While showing different images (like chickens pecking and apples on a branch) in her yard as well as images of trains and feet, *Espejo* cuts in and out of her testimonio (see her monologue—Appendix B). España, born and raised in an urban area, related to the rural or rancho influences through her cultural experience—she thinks she might be "a born again *ranchera*", therefore it comes as no surprise why she includes the chickens, apples and trains in this film that is an autobiographical portrait.

Done in 1991, *El Espejo* looks back at the trauma of España's childhood to see how social conditions of the past have affected not only her, but also the Chicana. While giving her testimonio, España addresses borders, boundaries and the politics of identity; she recalls a dream she once had:

> I was being beckoned the hell out of here so I jumped on a cloud that carried me across a sun-streaked sky and the air was filled with like giant bees, these moscas were telling me to get the hell out of East L.A. and one of them, one of them, spoke to me and said, "*Ay, Rosaurio, ¿Por dónde andas?*" And why the hell do you want to get out of this place girl, don't you know, you're already in wonderland. *Pues, fíjate, que volando así, charlando por todos, por todos lados estos* bees *y todos empezaron a chalar de la misma cosa que*

viví en wonderland that wonderland was the rock, that who did I think I was y *pa' acá y pa' aya y pa' acá y pa' ayá, y quien sabe que más, volaban así, charlando.* I tried to ignore all of it, you know, how it goes, but I was getting stung real bad and then even the country signs confirmed it, man, I lived in *maravilla.* I tried to wave goodbye, but by then it was too late. With the last long look back I saw them sealing everything up with this like invisible stuff, you know, like glue, gook, the people, the gente, the gente couldn't see it, but they couldn't see it beyond it. And you know all of this was just a dream, but then I couldn't finish it. They wouldn't let me come back; they wouldn't let me cross over until I showed them something. I needed some kind of documentation, I was an illegal, right, and it's like I couldn't make up unless I showed them my papers. Isn't that a trip? Oh God, figures. Well, anyway...volaban así, charlando, they still do it, even when I'm awake, you know, I can see them flying around, you know, you've got to show them this, you've got to show them that, you've got to show them something all the fucking time. It's disgusting (*El Espejo/The Mirror* 1991).

The fact that España was an "illegal" in a land that once belonged to Mexico is a source of anger. Also, here the tension in trying to fit in as "an American," but not being allowed in as such is obvious here in this reiteration of a dream sequence.

España's concerns in the film closely reflect the internal colonial model which explains how past social conditions have shaped the Chicana historical context. When the Southwest was taken by Anglos, the colonialism imposed thereafter was internal—meaning Chican@s are/were colonized within the boundaries of the mother country, the United States. They, therefore, live in an exploited condition (Barrea 485). In the United States, Chican@s exist in a society where they are powerless, one result of capitalism. Additionally, dominant nativist and ethnocentric ideas suppress Chican@ cultural practices. It is these types of social conditions that affect the Chicana and her triple oppression.

Through her film, España brings recognition to this internal colonialism. She first accomplishes this through the use of *testimonio* ". . . that situates the spectator as bearing witness to contestations of race, remembrance, and the ever-looming threat of cultural erasure" (Huaco-Nuzum 80). Through a testimonio, España is able to offer a more intimate and personal perspective, actively involving the spectator. Rosa Linda Fregoso also points this out in her book, *The Bronze Screen*:

>...*La Ofrenda*, [...] and *Espejo* involve a shift toward the 'aesthetics of reception' that de Lauretis makes reference to, 'where the spectator is the film's primary concern— primary in the sense that it is there from the beginning, inscribed in the filmmaker's project, and even in the very making of the film.' The visual and symbolic spaces organized by Chicana filmmakers re-vision Chicano aesthetic and formal knowledge because they define their points of identification with characters, images, and camera as "female, feminine, feminist." Rather than addressing a universal subject (spectator/viewer/audience), these [...] films, each in its own unique manner of expression, articulate the sites and forms of visions for an alternative social subject, mapping feminist identities, subjectivities,

and desires for U.S. Third World women of color." (*The Bronze Screen* 121)

Huaco-Nuzum further explains how España uses Chicana aesthetics to tell her story:
> España ventures into the private, intimate space where dreams are forged. She invites the spectator to witness her pain, her alienation, her anger, her accommodation. It is through this process of self-disclosure that España offers the spectator an opportunity to gain a new form of knowledge. In the end, the process of testimonio and bearing witness serves as bridge toward a better understanding and reconciliation between self, other, community and nation." (Huaco-Nuzum 90)

España backs up this idea in her article, "*On Filmmaking: A Personal Odyssey.*" Appealing to the Chicano aesthetic is important in her work. As she states:
> My experience speaks to life sobreviviendo the fracasos of beauty and brutal truth. It speaks to a Chicano aesthetic evolving from the fusion of contrasting dynamics within the Chicano experience. And ultimately, it speaks to one's faith in one's own vision of things, and in one's self, no matter what—*con safos* [...] It was several years before I realized that my aesthetics were as much a party to my vision as my ideas [...] My themes are themes of life; personal impressions of my own history, time and place—woven with humor and intellect. It is video art. (275-278)

This "video art" is evident in *El Espejo*. Creatively, España uses a fragmented body alternating shots of her feet and face to go along with her fragmented narrative:

"...an autobiographical account that mix memory and desire, reflection and projection, past and present reality and nightmarish dreams [reveal] the psychological trauma of cultural displacement" (Fitzsimons 20). Yet, Chon Noriega refutes the "psychological" part of the trauma of cultural displacement, and thinks, rather that it should be "historical" (163). Historical it is, for as Huaco-Nuzman states:

> The video is an homage to ancestors, family, culture and nation, pivoting between spatial realities that serve as ground and foreground to an examination of cultural trauma, social displacement and the (re)positioning of the Chicana subject. (83)

While the video is historical, its historical basis stems from the Chican@ heritage of colonialism that España uses to explain present social situations. Ultimately, the true meaning of the title in unveiled:

> España contests the nation's mirror by forcing the spectator to bear witness to a discourse that uncovers the nation's inability to accurately reflect and implement constitutional ideals for all citizens. España suggests that the desire to return to the past is a last-ditch attempt to retain cultural hegemony. (85)

Through the implementation of documentation, España is able to not only use *un espejo* (her reflections of her own childhood) to delve into her situation, but also she is able to address "the nation's mirror" by forcing the screener to look back on the reality of internal colonialism in the United States through España's eyes and voice. As España explains, "*El Espejo/The Mirror* is a concept based on ancient nahuatl philosophy, 'tú éres mi otro yo,' 'you are my other self'. The mirror is also referenced in its use by the ancient nahua sages who hold up the mirror so that we might see ourselves... reflection" (Personal Interview 5/16/04). By doing so, she gives Chicanas back their voice.

Chapter 10
Loving Pedro Infante (2001)

I love that woman.
—Denise Chávez of Tere
in *Loving Pedro Infante*

Denise Chávez's *Loving Pedro Infante* was published in 2001, 22 years after *Chicana*, more than 15 years after Cota-Cárdenas' *Puppet*, 13 years after *La Ofrenda*, and ten years after *Paletitas de Guayaba and El Espejo/The Mirror*. Although the time period between the first work discussed herein and this one is two decades, *Loving Pedro Infante* shows the same tendencies as all six works. That is, as a Chicana work, *Loving Pedro Infante* is an example of an act of liberation from the restraints of American society. The book tells the story of Teresina "Tere" Ávila, a teacher in her thirties and divorcée on the journey to discover herself. The novella "touches some real cords with women and relationships and trying to break free of dysfunctional relationships, [finding one's] way and [becoming] an empowered person" as a result (Personal Interview 5/10/04). Through the films in which Pedro Infante stars, Tere is able to find a passion for life that exists beyond Cabritoville, U.S.A. (Las Cruces, N.M.), where she lives. Chávez felt the need to write Tere's story because there are Teres and Irmas everywhere "waiting for that right person, Mr. Right or Ms. Right or whoever the right person is, to walk in the door and take [one] away from [that] boring life" (Personal Interview 5/10/04).

Chávez, in an interview with Annie O. Eysturoy, mentions very important aspects of her writing as a Chicana. Like Gonzáles-Berry, Chávez believes "[w]riting is a healing process" (Eysturoy 167), and that the healing process gives you a voice: "I am a transmitter of the woman's voice, a voice that may or may not have been heard; in the greater, larger world it has not been heard. And so I feel particularly close to many of my characters who are women" (165). Growing up in a household of all females, Chávez is very conscious of the silencing of women that has occurred over the years. As she points out:

> There are themes of interest to myself [...] for instance the changing relationship between men and women as women are coming into their own. Our grandmothers did not have voices. My mother's voice was a cry, perhaps, a moan; it was a sad voice. Our voices are hopefully stronger, and we can sing out stories and other women's stories as well. (Eysturoy 164)

Chávez's mother was a great influence and an important mentor for Chávez. And while there is no refuting that Chávez was not denied the female experience, growing up in a household of all women, she still recognized the silencing of her grandmother's and mother's voices by the surrounding community.

Therefore, it comes as no surprise that Chávez writes the book in first person narration, after all, "it's a first person kind of story [. . .] when you use first person that's a very immediate sensory experience and [*Loving Pedro Infante*] was her story and that's how she started talking" (Personal Interview 5/10/04). The narration is conversational in style (reflecting Chávez's theatre background), making the novel informal and therefore intimate—giving a voice to the protagonist. Chávez chooses to use a Chicana voice, Tere's voice, to relate sexual episodes and offer various intimate perspectives of sexuality. In the same 1990 interview Annie O.

Eysturoy asked Chávez what common themes could be found in her writing, she replied:

> Perhaps my concern is a woman of thirty-nine because number one, I am growing older. I feel comfortable with myself, I feel I am becoming the person I am; sexuality is a very important theme to me, relationships between men and women, women and women, men and men. Just looking at some of the myths of sex, and I don't mean just the act of making love, but like I said, the face of an angel; women are to be this, we are to harness ourselves [...] The fact is that if one enjoys any kind of sexuality, intimacy, for women it is immediately put into a certain category and we have this myth to deal with and these lies, really, these lies that we have lived with for so long. (167-168)

Chávez deliberately includes a substantial amount of sexual references, episodes and experience in her writing. In *Loving Pedro Infante*, these sexual references come from her affairs with Lucio in the Sands Motel in Cabritoville, U.S.A. For example, this is evident in one hilarious episode in which, La Tere, has to find and insert a diaphragm:

> I had to stop and say insistently to Lucio "*Querido*, wait a minute. Please, I have to put *La Cosa in*." I went into the other half room, the shame room, to put the Monster from Hell in before *mi querido* would have to see me [...] I hopped into the little room, moist breasts flopping. They were *sudosos* from Lucio's tongue, still full of his perspiration. One small dark wiry hair of his was wrapped around a nipple.
> Alien, I discovered to my dismay, was in the

glove compartment of my car, down the street near Sofia's Mighty Taco [...] I went to my car and got the damn pink holder [Upon returning] I stumbled across the room to my damn overnight case to where the damn Morrell's was and took out the damn Creature from Planet X [...] I limped back, took off my clothes and stood there, *chichis sueltas y caídas*, my breasts dead fish, my nipples slightly sore from Lucio's first crazy bites as I got back into bed. Lucio was out again and was snoring loudly.

I jellied the hell out of Rosemary's Baby, squeezing out the initial L for Lucio-Baby-I-can't-live-without-you-Papito-you're-the-only-one-really-the-only-one inside the plastic face. I folded the rim in, and tucked it into my body, a long standing battleground, where it tried to find merciful darkness. (94-96)

In this passage as well as others, the diaphragm[12382] is given various names, "el *Diablo*," "the Monster from Hell," "*La Cosa*," "the damn Creature from Planet X," "Rosemary's Baby," "*El Demonio*," and "*La Vieja*." These names are an example of Chávez's creative sexual and metaphorical humor when writing sexual passages. In fact, her humor is loaded with metaphorical references to the body. For instance, she describes her female genitalia as a hot *sopaipilla*, "Just watching him on the screen makes my little *sopaipilla* start throbbing underneath all the folds and tucks of cloth on the old and creaky theater seat, just give me some honey" (9). By making metaphorical humorous references to sexual organs and body parts, Chávez is able to not only free herself from the shackles of society, but also she is able to address issues of gender equality, not only within the Chicano community, but within greater American society as well. These issues are continuously addressed throughout the novel, and like those before her, namely Gonzáles-Berry and Cota-Cárdenas, Chávez takes in hand the issue of La Malinche and La Llorona:

> Sofia's was near the row of old cottonwoods that rimmed the small park by the river, near a tree-lined bend in the Río Grande where is was reputed La Llorona lived. The city fathers, currently a blustery, overfed, slightly constipated quorum of short older men, had named the spot Cortez Park last year in a citywide festival. The park honored Hernán Cortez, never mentioning, of course, his guide/translator/mistress, Doña Marina, La Malinche of the legend, *una vendida* who sold her people out to the Spanish conquerors. Ay, was the same act repeating itself? Was Lucio the conquistador and I the woman whose shame would go down through history? (92-93)

For an instant, La Tere compares her relationship with Lucio to La Malinche and Hernan Cortés, respectively. While Chávez does not recreate the myth of La Malinche like Cota-Cárdenas and Gonzáles-Berry, she does address how ludicrous Cortés' relationship was with Doña Marina. By pointing this out, Chávez is allowing the reader to understand how ridiculous the archetype of La Malinche really is, for Malinche was the slave sold to Cortés by her own family, Malinche had no other option than to obey Cortés, unless she wanted to suffer the consequences for not doing so. The hypocrisy really lies with the myth— the women are innocent yet they are ultimately the ones punished.

Perhaps the reason why Chávez does not reinvent the Malinche myth is because she decides to address the more prominent archetypes of today's Chican@ society—that being "*puta*", a.k.a the Big P. Referring to a smaller Cabritoville, but alluding to the greater Chican@ community, Chávez writes in the voice of La Tere: "When you 'play the field' in Cabritoville, the field is pretty rough terrain. After a while, you're branded with a Big A, or in my culture, a Big P, for *Puta*" (46). In fact, "La gran P" can be a number of things—*Pendeja, Pioja, Puta, Pelada*—all with connections to the letter P (15). By mentioning this, Chávez is making a statement about how she feels about such references. She equates the label of "*puta*" imposed on women by Chican@ culture to being branded—"*puta*" is literally burned on to you and will be with you for the rest of your life. In order to achieve a new identity for the Chicana, Chicana writers must eliminate the extremes from la puta to la virgen. In so doing, they affirm the experience of the Chicana and the potency of the Chicana. Chávez does this by adding tidbits, like "*Puta Power*" (19)—demystifying the traditional connotations associated with such a word. Because *Loving Pedro Infante* came out 15 years after *Puppet*, there is this change in archetypal figures or labels. Obviously through the past 15 years, the idea of puta has become more evident first in *Paletitas de gGuayaba*, and later in *Loving Pedro Infante*.

As a Chicana, Chávez takes the opportunity to poke fun at the common misnomers of self-reference that her fellow Chicanas have made. For example, when La Tere mentions her Spanish *Tocaya* (69), St. Teresa de Ávila, she manages to go to the sublime and ridiculous with a list (69-71) of how La Tere and St. Teresa de Ávila are and are not similar. It is then that Chávez pokes fun at Castilian Spanish. In fact there are several references to the Castilian dialect in the novel: "*Una Ethpañola*" (69) and "*El ethpañol*" (156). Chávez writes "*español*" as "*ethpañol*" to parody the "s" of the Castilian dialect—the "s" is different in Castillian Spanish than in Mexican/Chican@ dialect of

Spanish—it is an alveolar rather than a dental S. Chávez mocks Castilian Spanish here. Chávez explains:
"Oh, oh the "ethpañol" because that's how the Spanish people talk. People talk that way, I mean I'm exaggerating; I'm playing and having fun with people's language. So I mean, you know, you just have to play, writing is play, can't we play? [L]et's face it, I live in the south, people in the northern part of New Mexico, they're very Spanish, sometimes they look down on Mexicans and the people that live in this part of the world. But, you know, I don't have time for that either, that's other people's problems. But you can also always poke a little fun and deflate egos, why not? (Personal Interview 5/10/04)

Chávez does not think the Castilian dialect inferior, because within the Chican@ community, the Castilian dialect is associated with being Spanish and therefore European which implies a hierarchy to Mexican with indigenous roots. Really, it comes back to the basic racial issues of white and black. White being Spanish and black being the Mexican indigenous heritage—white is considered superior within American society and for many Chican@s who have not been taught otherwise, they think that the Castilian dialect is superior. This feeling of inferiority is perpetuated by Anglos and also by Chican@s who choose to belittle themselves for their dialectal differences from Castillian Spanish. Gloria Anzaldúa makes this point clearer when she states, "As a culture, we call ourselves Spanish when referring to ourselves as a linguistic group and when copping out. It is then that we forget our predominant Indian genes" (62). La Tere experiences this copping out by three Chicanos during a visit to Santa Fe. She described the Chican@s as:
. . .Santa Fe-style dudes a 'lo todo La

Conquistador in the plaza. You know the type: I'm Spanish. You're Mexican. The Mexican in them had invited us to go dancing at La Fonda while the Spanish part kept looking at us sideways like we were inferior human beings. (185)

In fact, anyone denying the Mexican part of their Chican@ identity annoys La Tere: "I hate that north/south shit. The northerners can't understand that the Spaniards came up through Méjico. Who do they think they had babies with? What are we but a *mestizaje*, a mixture of all the people in the world?" (186). Chávez is sending a message to *La Raza* here—not to deny your roots, because in so doing you deny and reject your true identity.

Chávez's Spanish, in *Loving Pedro Infante*, is more similar to the kind Gonzáles-Berry describes—a variety of codes. And while Chávez does not use choose to write her novel in Spanish, she does include little morsels of code-switching (without translation) through the text, for example, "Like *queso fundido con moscas*" (40). By including these key phrases she identifies with *La Raza*—as a bilingual woman, Chávez allows her true identity to ring clear and that happens with her English voice, her Spanish voice and her code-switching voice and a combination of all three. She does not conform to the English-only rules of the majority of American society. She is a multi-lingual/dialectal woman and conveys that in her writing. By doing this, she, gives the reader a sense of Chicanisma and gives Chicanas a name, voice and image.

Chapter 11
Conclusion

To be revolutionary is to be original,
  to know where we came from,
to validate what is ours and help it
  to flourish,
the best of what is ours, of our
  beginnings, our principles,
and to leave behind what no longer
  serves us.
—Inés Hernández,
Chicana political activist

Through the narratives of *Puppet, Paletitas de Guayaba,* and *Loving Pedro Infante* by Margarita Cota-Cárdenas, Erlinda Gonzáles-Berry and Denise Chávez, and the films, *Chicana, La Ofrenda: The Days of the Dead* and *El Espejo/ The Mirror* by Sylvia Morales, Lourdes Portillo and Susana Muñoz, and Frances Salomé España, respectively, Chicanas are given their rightful name, voice and image. This is done through the sense of Chicanisma, a (re)discovery and (re)presentation of Chicana history and culture, that the works project.

These works provide a more realistic look into historical, cultural and societal portrayals of the Chicana experience. Considering that six of the seven[12383] artists are either first or second generation Chicanas and were some way directly or indirectly involved in the Chicano Movement—Morales and Portillo in their filmmaking, España in MEChA and Mujer, Gonzáles-Berry by starting a *"Mujer Chicana"* class at the University of New Mexico, Cota-Cárdenas by helping to start the first Chicano Studies

Latina Filmakers & Writers 115

program at her college in California and Chávez through her theatre—it is no surprise that they (re)present the Chicana and her triple colonization in some way or another in their works.

Through the venues of film and literature, these filmmakers and writers are able to confront the triple oppression they face in American society—that of race, class and gender. The films and books challenge Anglo, Chicano and Mexican norms of society. They address many issues, racial and cultural, such as creations of myths, nativism, internal colonialism, cultural deprivation and homosexuality that are ignored by Hollywood films and mainstream literature. Ultimately, by reconstructing fact, truth and history through film and literature, they are able to finally give Chicanas their rightful voice, name and image.

The rightful voice, image and name provided by these works for, by and about but not limited to Chicanas are ones that do not subjugate, oppress or marginalize her existence. In the past, Chicanas have had little control over their self-image and self-definition due to the fact that many books and films that gave them an image, voice and name were created and written by males, especially Anglo males that created stereotypical images and names. Nowadays, Chicanas and Latinas, like Sylvia Morales, Margarita Cota-Cárdenas, Lourdes Portillo and Susana Muñoz, Erlinda Gonzáles-Berry, Frances Salomé España and Denise Chávez, through their works use film and literature to portray a more accurate depiction of themselves.

While these works call for social justice, they more so communicate the Chicana experience in American society. They look at relationships (Morales, Chávez and Cota-Cárdenas all mention in their interviews included in the appendices that they look at relationships in their works) within the Chican@/Latin@ community and between the

Chican@/Latin@ community and other American and Mexican communities. This new vision re-writes gender issues across Chican@ and Mexican borders as well as other American racial/ethnic boundaries. These filmmakers and authors make these films for all audiences—they are not exclusionists, but inclusionists. Even if they principally make them for themselves, they ultimately want to share them with everyone and not be limited to one audience—otherwise they would not be published and available to the public—the entire public—any race, class or gender.

Their (re)presented female vision delivers new insight about language and identity because it flies in the face of mainstream patriarchal culture, language and identity. The patriarchal family is a social space that is typically scrutinized and deconstructed in Chicana work because it positions women in subordinate and marginal spheres (Rosaura Sánchez 54). These Chicanas, *mejicanas*, *nuevamejicanas*, and Latinas illustrate that code-switching (commonly known as Spanglish) is not only a cultural identity, but a phenomenon of border culture and communities. They illustrate that Chicanas are products of American society—they've been marginalized, subjugated and oppressed, yet continue to fight for their rights following the Chicano Movement, the Women's Liberation Movement and the Chicana Feminist Movement. They illustrate different subjects in their works, often taboo subjects.

None of these works is exactly like the other nor does one closely resemble another, especially because many of the works represent the time in which they were written. However, what these works do have are common attempts to alleviate Chicanas from their subordinate position in society. The evolution of these works is inspiring and encouraging. From *Chicana* in 1979 to *Loving Pedro Infante* in 2001, 22 years have passed. Yet, themes in these works have in many ways stayed similar.

The current plight of the Chicana does not stray far from what Sylvia Morales tried to overcome 25 years ago with *Chicana*—sexism and education. The most important issue for artists, critics, filmmakers and authors is "to stress the human aspects, what are commonalities, and that way bring about more understanding and cohesion instead of division" (Portillo, Personal Interview, 5/10/04). Understanding of one another in and out of our own culture is what will bring social justice. The first step is education, and these works educate readers and viewers about the Chicana's human condition in Chican@ and the greater American society.

This (re)discovery of Chicana history has already led to a change in filmmaking, film studies, in literature, and literary studies—comparing *Loving Pedro Infante* to *Chicana*—it is apparent that Chávez now makes subtle references to the Chicana condition compared to what Morales does in *Chicana*. Also, as España explains:

> The first waves of Chicana artists and intellectuals have provided a legacy which manifests in a very empowered and dynamic younger generation of Chicana artists. The good part is that there exists a possibility for communication and creative exchange between the generations of artists whose works express an evolving Chicana aesthetic [...] Of course it is not the same as 30 years ago [either]. The legacy of that time is present in a whole new generation of activists who are extremely informed and dedicated to social change, and spiritual growth, many of whom are young women artists who demonstrate this commitment in their work, in their art. (Personal Interview 5/16/04)

Not only have first waves of Chicanas provided a legacy,

but later works by first wave Chicanas are not like their earlier works. That is, for example, Chávez can write differently now than she did in the early 1970s. Chávez is no longer obligated to explain the references she makes, but rather use them to expand on the Chicana experience—to empower. Likewise, "subsequent generations have had access to this knowledge and are not only benefiting from this foundation but are expanding on this base of knowledge and expression in significant ways" (España Personal Interview 5/16/04). "Many of us, and certainly young women today hold on the same basic tenets: the necessity to struggle against injustice and to empower our mujeres, our people and our communities through both our intellectual and our political work" (Gonzáles-Berry Personal Interview 4/13/04).

This new vision re-writes gender issues across borders because it brings to the attention of many the gender oppression faced by Chicanas as sexual beings. Already since *Chicana*, it has helped yield new special practice— the Church does not have its walls surrounding each Chicana anymore. Sure, she is still restricted, but she is more able to express herself and choose what she wants to do with her body—and understands it is her choice, not someone else's. Of course, there are still bridges to be built and crossed—both Chicana film and literature have been studied by scholars, but this is the first time six works have been studied side by side and similar conclusions among all six works have been drawn.

This (re)presented female vision gives us new insight about language and identity—different dialects of Spanish are being accepted since they are being published, read and watched. Likewise, Chicanas are allowed to be themselves and to feel empowered and to be proud of their heritage, their history and their culture. In the words of Frances Salomé España:

> Being a Chicana any time means we have to struggle against encumbrances and oppression of all kinds: sexism, *Machismo*, racism, social injustice and inequities, not to mention the obstacles that still remain when confronting the main stream, i.e., for the most part they still don't even know we exist. (Personal Interview 5/16/04)

Yet, with each new study and each new work, the Chicana voice is stronger and is becoming *más fuerte*.

APPENDIX A

THE CHICANO
El Chicano
Por Lalo Guerrero

Yo soy Chicano, Señores
Nací al lado Americano
Para México soy pocho
No me aceptan mis hermanos

Los gringos me discriminan
Como si fuera extranjero
A pesar de que esta tierra
Fue de México primero

Este país es mi tierra
México es la de mis padres
Pero la sangre que llevo
Es la de Benito Juárez

Yo soy purito Chicano
De raza que no se raja
Mi madre nació en Sonora
Mi padre fue de la Baja

Mis padres me inculcaron
Su cultura desde chavo
No es mi culpa haber nacido

Al otro lado del Bravo

*Me da mucho sentimiento
Que en México no me quieran
Porque a México lo quiero
Lo quiero más que a mi tierra*

*Como Emiliano Zapata
Y también Francisco Villa
Yo soy revolucionario
En este moderno día*

*Unidos a Cesar Chávez
Los México-Americanos
Luchamos por la justicia
Para todo el Mexicano*

*Por mi educación bilingüe
Hablo Chicano y gabacho
Ya se despide este pocho
Hasta luego y hay los guacho*

APPENDIX B

EL ESPEJO/THE MIRROR TESTIMONIO(1991)
Testimonio[12384]
 I mean, I wasn't so bad, things were actually quite clear then, you know. Heaven was the sky and hell was somewhere...under the dirt, you know. It was pretty clear, but I was, I couldn't have been that bad, people survived, you know.
 But, I was always in the trees, so I was very safe. That this place has a corazón unto itself, you know, something very special, something that we had to learn to embrace.
 What a beautiful thing, trying to figure that one out, you know, that we drew our breaths from an urban area, something far removed and yet so close to the homeland, you know.
 I was being beckoned the hell out of here so I jumped on a cloud that carried me across a sun-streaked sky and the air was filled with like giant bees, these moscas were telling me to get the hell out of East L.A. and one of them, one of them, spoke to me and said, "Ay, Rosaurio, ¿por dónde andas?" And why the hell do you want to get out of this place girl, don't you know, you're already in wonderland. Pues, fíjate, que volando asi, charlando por todos, por todos lados estos bees y todos empezaron a chalar de la misma cosa que viví en wonderland that wonderland was the rock, that who did I think I was y pa' acá y pa' ayá y pa' acá y pa' ayá, y quién sabe que más, volaban así, charlando. I tried to ignore all of it, you know, how it goes, but I was getting stung real bad and then even the country signs confirmed it, man, I lived in maravilla. I tried to wave

goodbye, but by then it was too late. With the last long look back I saw them sealing everything up with this like invisible stuff, you know, like glue, gook, the people, the gente, the gente couldn't see it, but they couldn't see it beyond it. And you know all of this was just a dream, but then I couldn't finish it. They wouldn't let me come back; they wouldn't let me cross over until I showed them something. I needed some kind of documentation, I was an illegal, right, and it's like I couldn't make up unless I showed them my papers. Isn't that a trip? Oh God, figures. Well, anyway. . .volaban así, charlando, they still do it, even when I'm awake, you know, I can see them flying around, you know, you've got to show them this, you've got to show them that, you've got to show them something all the fucking time. It's disgusting.

APPENDIX C
INTERVIEW WITH SYLVIA MORALES
Chicana (1979)
Personal/Career Questions:

JD: What is your upbringing? Where/how were you raised? (With this question I am more or less interested in knowing how you got involved in filmmaking)

SM: I was born in Phoenix, AZ. Early influence was playing to the radio in front of my brothers and sisters. Younger siblings are a great audience as you're growing up. We didn't have enough money for a television so we'd sit around the radio, and I would argue with whoever was talking on the radio. My siblings would crack up at whatever I did or said. Besides them my grandmother and aunts were a great audience for my singing and dancing. I loved an audience. We also went every weekend to the Mexican cinema when we lived in Los Angeles. I loved the drama of Mexican cinema and the huge black and white pictures of the movie stars of my mother's day in the lobby of the Million Dollar movie palace. María Felix, Pedro Infante, Leticia Palma, Luis Aguilar, Pedro Amendariz, etc.

JD: How do you identify yourself (that is, Chicana, Hispana, etc)?

SM: Chicana, American, Mejicana but definetly not Hispanic.

JD: Why?

SM: I was raised being conscious of my heritage because my mother was aware of the racism I might encounter so she instilled pride in my heritage. I find the word 'Hispanic' generic, bland without sustenance.

JD: Do you consider yourself a feminist?
SM: Yes.

JD: Could you expand on it please?
SM: Actually, it's quite apparent that I'm a feminist from my movie *Chicana*. The movie depicts the oppression that Mexican women endured and celebrates those women who struggled for the vote, education, property rights and for the rights of men as well. So feminism is struggling for the rights of all human beings, in particular those who are the most oppressed, children, women, people of color (women & men). It's an eternal struggle.

JD: Right. Okay, well, I agree, but it is always interesting to hear how someone will describe it.

JD: Are you a religious person?
SM: No.

JD: What effects did the church and/or your family have on you growing up?
SM: As a child, I reached out to the Church because my home life was chaotic. I reached out to something that gave me a sense of values and something I felt would ground me. I know that in retrospect. I didn't know this as a child. As a child I went to where it seemed to be safe. However, I do not consider myself a Catholic—more a cultural Catholic. I love the visual theatricality of the Church.

JD: How about as a woman?
SM: My mother tried hard to give me a strong sense of self but was herself caught up in a male-centered culture.

Today I would say I am family centered, not necessarily nuclear family. Children are important and must feel good about who they are as they are growing up into adults.

JD: What languages did you speak growing up?
SM: Spanish and English.

JD: Which do you speak now?
SM: Both but English is easier since it is my first language.

JD: Would you rather I conduct this interview in Spanish?
SM: No.

JD: Growing up did you have a role model?
SM: My mother in the early years and, for better or worse, my tías, Alicia and Olga, and then my Uncle Robert (my mother's brother), then later Ida Lupino who was a director in film and María Félix (Mexican actress).

JD: What about a Chicana role model? How about now, do you have a role model?
SM: Role models today are those women who have been and are successful at resisting what is oppressive and have survived. I also admire the beautiful works that people do—be they art, films, architecture, literature, activism in the community.

JD: Okay, moving on to something different—what filmmakers/directors and/or film critics have been influential to you? And how come?
SM: I believe everything has influenced me in my life. For better or for worse. I do know that I love particular movies because they moved me or they stayed with me, I love movies that make me laugh out loud. Really make

you laugh, like, *Freaky Friday*. I love movies that tear me up inside and force me to think or rethink issues. Movies that stir things up. These movies have the gift of giving one an insight into the human condition. That means that first there was a script, a producer, then a director, a director of photography, the actors, composer, music director and everyone else who works on a movie set or a television set. They've all affected me. Very specifically, I love Orsen Wells. His *Woman from Shanghai* with Rita Hayworth, there's a very famous mirror scene in it. *Citizen Kane*, of course, and *A Touch of Evil*. Also, *Algiers* I saw it when I was a kid, and it stars Hedy Lamarr, Charles Boyer and was directed by John Cromwell. A very romantic movie. I paid homage to the last scene in this movie in a movie I made at the Directing Workshop for Women at the AFI. My movie, though, dealt with children so the end happened to children instead of adults.

JD: Wow—

SM: I love John Houston, his *Sierra Madre*, *Asphalt Jungle*. There's a movie, Australian movie, called, *High Tide* that is a mother daughter relationship movie. It's a favorite. Judy Davis stars—she's great, I love her. I love the Italians! Bertolucci with his *The Conformist*. Fellini, he's another favorite with his *8 ½*, Visconte, Lucino Visconte, Sergio Leone, of whom, Tarantino, an American Italian, has played homage to in his latest *Kill Bill*.

JD: Yes.

SM: Sergio Leone did *Once Upon a Time in America*, *Once Upon a Time in the West*, *A Fist Full of Dollars*. Bergman with *Cries and Whispers*, did you ever see *Cries and Whispers*?

JD: No...

SM: Ah! Okay, the Wachowski brothers with *Bound*

starring Gina Gershon and Jennifer Tilly. The Wachowski brothers also did *Matrix*. Another fabulous movie maker is Woody Allen with *Annie Hall*, *Bullets Over Broadway*, you've gotta see *Bullets Over Broadway*. *Crimes and Misdemeanors*. The Mexicans, María Novaro with *Danzón*. *Amores Perros*, you've seen that?

JD: Yes.

SM: Okay, so you know, and the Japanese, they've got incredible filmmakers. Okay, most recent, *28 Days Later* makes great use of digital. I loved *Mulholland Drive* though on first viewing found it confusing. But emotionally it was haunting and the feelings of loss were so intense and dark—really disturbed me. I love to be swept away by a movie. And, you know, that's what profound love will do. It will sweep you away. And great movies are like love, they have the power to sweep you away...so influence, every great movie has influenced me and some of them in a way that I pay homage to if I get a chance to express it. I could go on and on...

JD: Yes...have you continued to create films on Chican@ themes?

SM: I was part of a series called *Chicano! The Mexican-American Civil Rights Movement*. I did the farm worker's struggle.

JD: Oh, neat!

SM: So I have continued to work in it when able to, for instance I directed many of the episodes from Showtime's dramatic series called *Resurrection Blvd*. It's about a Chicano family in East Los Angeles involved in the boxing business. It's about a family's ups and downs who happen to be Chicano. I feel I can direct other themes and topics and pretty much anything. I may be hired to do a subject

I'm not crazy about—my challenge then becomes to find what's meaningful or exciting in it and get a hold of it somehow. I've done that. We're not always going to get something we necessarily want to do...sometimes you've just got to work to bring home the frijoles. I've got to pay the rent, and I have two children to support.

JD: Right, gotcha. So if you had your choice, is the Chicano relationship to the dominant culture something you'd like to explore in filmmaking?

SM: I guess my preference would be to do stories from my culture but not necessarily in relation to the dominant culture. I'm interested in the relations Chicanos or Latinos have between themselves and everything else that can occur to anybody or any family. Right now I'm working on a funded treatment. Guess what? My lead is a Chicana, but it's not about a Chicano subject. She's a Chicana. Another character in the same story is a Mexican woman who is here illegally with her two children. And another character is a Cuban.

JD: Does anyone in your family make films or tell stories; I mean how did you get into filmmaking, why did you want to be a director?

SM: I love an audience. And good stories hold people's attention—if you can hold people's attention, that means you're telling a good story or a good joke, so you're doing something that's right because they keep looking at you, or they keep looking at your movie or at your artwork—do you see what I'm saying? I love putting on a good performance, a good show, I love the process of putting something together that works and pleases an audience. Where did I get that? I have no idea. Perhaps because in a large family you have to work to get attention. Who knows?

JD: Would you say there is a common theme present in all your work?

SM: Family relations and relationships. I'm interested in women's place in the world. If I worked on the script then the woman's role is significant. Her struggle with love, family, siblings, and the things life throws at her.

JD: So, as a woman, as a Chicana, did you have a difficult time getting into the film world?

SM: It's still difficult. It helps a great deal if you know people in the business, particularly those who have hiring power. I don't have friends in powerful positions.

I have a great mentor. We're the same age. He's the kind of individual who is interested in bringing in more Latinos to the business. He's a director but directors don't get to hire unless they're staff directors. Or you have to be the writer/producer or, you know, the head of the studio, something like that. If he was in a hiring position I'd be working steadily. He's really pushed for me. He's the one that got me work on *Resurrection Blvd*. One has to make those connections early on... that's what we're actually trying to do right now—build some sort of infrastructure in the business and get more Latinos in positions of hiring.

Questions about *Chicana*:

JD: Moving on to questions specifically about *Chicana*. Have you worked on it since it came out in '79?

SM: No, but I'm considering updating it.

JD: Yeah, I think it would be great. (NOTE: As of July 2005 SM has begun doing research for CHICANA2)

JD: What inspired you to make *Chicana* in the first place?

SM: I got a flyer that Anna Nieto-Gómez was going to be presenting a slide show at this place called, I think it was called, The Inner City Cultural Center in Los Angeles, and I wanted to be supportive because I knew her from UCLA. She presented a wonderful slide show aimed at working-class Latinas, encouraging them to strike. So it must have been to a very specific group of working women, I don't recall. This was sometime in '77 or '78. Within this strike slide show she was showing, there was this history that I had never known about, about Mexican women. It was a goldmine of information plus it had a powerful feminist point of view with which I was in complete agreement. I was moved and excited.

I talked to her afterwards and told her I'd love to adapt here slideshow into a movie. I wasn't interested in the strike aspect, which was one of the important points in her slide show. I was interested in her research. I would later add to that research with my own. She was excited that I would want to make a movie on something she had worked on.

Cindy Honesto, a friend of hers who had helped her with her slide show assisted me in the research I would be gathering. Cindy was a great help. Cindy had apparently shot a lot of those slides for Anna. So Anna asked Cindy to help me locate photos Cindy had shot from books.

JD: Oh really, that's wonderful!
SM: Yeah, my brothers, my sister, mom, who is now 80 years old, all appear in the movie. I produced it, shot it, did the sound and edited. It was 1978—I had dropped out of school for a few years and returned to make *Chicana*. Everyone I knew in the film school before I dropped out was gone—I didn't know a soul. And I didn't feel comfortable enough asking anybody for help. I almost had a mini nervous breakdown—you know, it's really hard to put a movie together even with help from people you know but by yourself—it becomes a Herculean task. Good thing it was a small movie. It's actually the only thing I

could have done by myself.

JD: WOW!

SM: When Anna came to see it, she couldn't believe it. She was very moved, "...You made it come alive!" those were her words to me. Of course, film does that, if you have good material and tell the story right...

JD: Yes.

SM: That's what inspired me—I saw this history with a political point of view I completely felt at home with and I wanted to tell that story in a movie so that others could see it and be blown away like I was. I saw Anna's slide show, and I knew I had to do it and I could adapt it to a movie.

JD: So, you already kind of answered this, because you've been thinking about it...do you think 24-25 years after its debut, there is anything you would change about it to bring it up to speed? Do you think it still applies today?

SM: I think it stands up pretty well. Its low-tech look makes it technically dated. But the storytelling still stands up. The political attitude still stands up. Actually, I looked at it a couple of nights ago with my 10 ½ year-old daughter. She thought it was "cool." I think I cut it too short in some scenes—since it was film (16mm), I cut it on a movieola, and it was difficult to tell what it would look like until you had already printed it—by then, of course, it's too late. Not like today when you can check everything out before deciding to print because of digital editing. Everything was linear when I did it. But it's still a strong piece of work. Thanks to Anna Nieto-Gómez, Carmen Moreno (wrote the original score) and Carmen Zapata (narrator).

JD: So your ultimate goal in making film, was to portray...?

SM: Was to let people know what Chicanas/Mexicanas had contributed historically to the culture and to put out a feminist take on that history. There was a film that was done 10 years before called...—

JD: *I am Joaquín?*

SM: Yeah! And when I saw that—I mean, it's a beautiful poem—and I know Luis Valdez, an actor (as well as a director), and he performed it with lots of feeling. But my objection at the time was that the only mention of women was something about "brown eyes." I didn't think "I'm going to make a movie in response to this exclusion..." I was disappointed but I was also moved by *Joaquín*. It's an emotional piece and works on its own level.

JD: Yes, I agree. You know that, I am assuming that you know, *Chicana* and *I am Joaquín* have been compared by Chon Noriega and Rosa Linda Fregoso?

SM: I know—they're seen as book ends. They've been compared and contrasted. The comparison mostly, I believe is that we both used the art of Mexican masters to tell our stories. I believe for both of us it was a matter of no budget. Also we're celebrating our culture. However, I didn't consciously make *Chicana* as a response to *Joaquín*. I made it because the historical aspects that Nieto-Gómez presented moved me. It motivated me to get the word out about our history.

JD: Prior to seeing Anna's slide show—what sort of relationship did you have with Anna?

SM: How do you mean?

JD: I mean, how did you know to go to the slide show?

SM: I received a flyer announcing the slide show as I mentioned because I knew her and I wanted to support her. I had heard her lecture at school and I liked what she said politically about women and how she said it.

JD: Yeah, I love the stuff that she's written... Do you know where *Chicana* has been seen primarily?
SM: In colleges, and I think it's used for film classes, Chicano Studies' classes.

JD: Well, the reason I asked that is because I wanted to know if they were Chicano organizations—
SM: For the most part they were Chicano organizations and organizations that had interests in Chicano, Black, Asian and American Indian studies.

JD: So do you think the film had any affect on the politics of inclusion within the movement after it screened? What were other writings, arts, and culture that also brought the Chicana's point of view into the debate?
SM: I don't know—I do think that it made Chicanas and Latinas feel good about themselves and brought a certain consciousness about the subject. As for other works, I don't know. I haven't really followed Chicano Studies. This was a movie that I had to make. I had a mission—I felt proud about the history and wanted the political point of view presented. If a subject I come across catches my passion, I'll do everything I can to make it happen and make it happen in a way that gets attention.

JD: Good for you. So how was the film received by the movement itself?
SM: It was very well received. People still rent it. It's always gotten a good response. I think there were only two times when I received a negative response. One was a young woman, a Chicana. She asked me why I had used the Mexican Masters to tell the story of Chicanas or Mexican women,—Orozco, Rivera, Siquieros. Why had I

used male artists to tell this story? Why didn't I use an artist like Frida Kahlo?—Well, first of all Frida Kahlo's work didn't lend itself to the story of Chicana. And again, this is the material that was available to tell a no budget movie. And I still feel the material works on so many levels despite, what feels to me, Rivera's over use of big breasted women. For me, it's fitting that I used these master works to tell about Chicana/Mexicana political history. It's kind of subversive, in a way. So she, the critic, agreed with me many years later.

The other comment dealt with the pre-Columbian artwork in *Chicana*. A professor in pre-Columbian art informed me that I hadn't used all the pre-Columbian art in its proper era. She lectured me in front of the audience. When she was done, I thanked her for her comments and I asked her if she would work as the expert on my next movie. She laughed, and she came up afterwards and said that she really loved the movie and would love to work with me (Laughing)—so those are the only two negative responses I have ever gotten. There may have been more—I never heard them.

JD: Are you surprised that someone like me is interested in it after 24/25 years?

SM: I am, and I'm pleased. I'm surprised, but pleasantly surprised. That's why I take the time to do this [the interview], to talk to you because I think it's great that you're doing this—to keep it alive. And I'm always thinking that I've got to do an update. I feel the story telling, the information, the humor still stands up. I mean, I could have gone on and on, but I needed to cut it—it's only 22 minutes—it's a survey with a definite political point of view! And it's entertaining.

JD: Yep...so when you say it is a "survey" would you not say it was a "documentary"?

SM: Well, it's a survey because it's historical and it's chronological and short—I go back to pre-Columbian times—a documentary I always think of as live, something that happens now, that is happening now right before your eyes...so maybe I'm being too literal. I have mixed in fictional characters with the participation of my family.

JD: Do you think that through films like *Chicana*, that U.S. Society will be more accepting of each other?

SM: You mean another culture being more accepting of Chicano culture?

JD: Yes.

SM: I don't know maybe—that wasn't the intent. I think there are films that will make you look a second time, for those who are open to looking. No matter what you show them, people have to be ready and willing to look. And if they are willing and ready and if something touches them, then they'll open up more.

JD: Right, I agree!

JD: As you know, I've included *Chicana* as a part of the Chicana works I am studying—I classify these works as works by, about and for Chicanas—would you agree?

SM: Yes, Chicanas were intended as my first row—if you're thinking of an audience, my first row was Chicanas. Chicanas, look at your history, be proud. My second row was Chicanos. Chicanos look at us, your sister, your mothers, your history, be proud. And then the other rows were anyone else that wanted to know about Chicanas, come on in. What fun, huh?

JD: Yes. I like that description.

JD: Also with the works I'm studying, I claim that *Chicana* as well as the other two films and three books are examples of what I've labeled Chicanisma. Ana Castillo talks about Xicanisma in her book, *Massacre of the Dreamers*. My idea of Chicanisma is—the concept of sisterhood—that it's Chicana artists that give Chicanas a name, a voice and an image. One that is different than that has been portrayed by males.

SM: I was conscious of one thing with regard to *I am Joaquín*. That I would not exclude males from *Chicana* the way women had been excluded from *Joaquín*. One can't exclude men or women from a history of a people. If you do, you only tell half of the story.

JD: You kind of offer a retelling of La Malinche in the film, I was wondering, was that a part of Anna's slide show? Or why did you think it was important to include that.

SM: I don't remember specifics but most likely it was in her slide show. I already knew about Malinche, her real name was Malitzin, and was quite taken by her story and there are variations to the story but either story you go by —she got raw deal. Malinche was a child when she was sold into slavery—she couldn't have been more than 12 or 13 or maybe younger—which means being a female slave, she was probably raped. When she's around 15 or 16, she's sold or traded to the Spanish. She's so brilliant she already knows a few languages, that's the main reason she was a good trade for the Spanish or Cortés, and she becomes Cortés' concubine and translator. She dies at 18 or 21.

So the story goes that she was called "La Malinche" by the Mexican Indians or Aztecs or "Leader". Later, it took the meaning of traitor. She's also known as "la Chingada", which literally means, "the fucked one"— so if someone calls you "hija or hijo de la chingada" – they're calling you a son of a bitch or son of the fucked one. And here she is, a slave, first to some tribe and then to the Spanish. What choices does she have? This adolescent is accused of selling out Mexico. How is this possible? Somebody that was powerless, who was a slave? Who braved who? It's a fascinating story. It's an important story in the history of Mexico. A baby she may have had by a Spaniard. I haven't kept up with the most current philosophical thinking in Mexico, so I don't know if this reading of Malinche still holds as it did when *Chicana* was made. I do know that she will always be a kind of tragic figure.

General Chican@ Questions:

JD: Moving onto more general Chican@ questions...Where you at all involved in the Chicano Movement?

SM: I was involved as a filmmaker. I did camera work on a television series—ABC, KABC in Los Angeles. I shot 13 half hour documentaries on the Chicano community. Yeah, I was involved as a filmmaker documenting what was going on.

JD: Okay. What was it like being a Chicana during those years?

SM: My family moved to East Los Angeles (which was almost totally Chicano), to the westside of Los Angeles, Culver City, in the mid 50's. At that time Culver City was totally white and Jewish. My mom said to me "Mija, some people are going to ask you if you're Spanish. Well, you're not Spanish, you're Mexican. And some people will call you a dirty Mexican, well you're Mexican, but you're not dirty. So don't let anyone push you around." So I was walking around school all the time with this big chip on my shoulder—daring people just to say something to me— because what my mom told me felt like was a warning. And I was aware of this difference because my mom made me aware. No one ever said anything to me that was racist at school.

And as an adult, I was aware of racism, definitely,

although I think I was more aware of sexism than I was of racism, but I wouldn't accept either one at that time or at least of what I was aware. I wouldn't let anyone disabuse me or be disrespectful to me.

JD: Where is your mom from and where is your dad from?

SM: My mom and father were both born in Mexico. So, I'm first generation.

JD: At what point did they move to the U.S.?

SM: Well, my mom was a baby, and my father I don't know because they divorced when I was a year old, and I never knew him.

JD: Oh, I'm sorry to hear that.

SM: No problem, I don't know what I'm missing.

JD: (Laughing) Do you have any brothers and sisters?

SM: I do, I have two brothers and three sisters from a second marriage so and I'm the oldest.

JD: Do you believe the Chicano and the Chicana Movement is still alive today? And do think it will ever die?

SM: Well, the Chicano Movement as it was, no, is not alive. But I think there's a lot of activity in a different way. For example, I just saw some student films, where I teach, at Loyola Marymout University. One was done by a young man named Junior Gonzáles and the other one was done by a young woman named April Lopez. And this was done on a campus that doesn't by any means have a large Latino population. They were excellent and they weren't about the Chicano movement or racism. They were relationship stories and they were powerful.

Chicanos from my generation were concerned about

identity and wanted people to know who Chicanos were. Today, the field is wider. Identity, comedy, mystery, sexuality—everything is up for grabs as far as subject matter. What they film could be about anyone—it just so happens to be about someone who happens to be Chicano. It's great. They're expressing their art, what they feel about the human condition.

JD: What is the current plight of the Chican@ in your opinion, and do you think it's changed since *Chicana* was made?

SM: Well, I think the lack of access to a goal education hurts us. I believe that the poor and uneducated and underclass are getting blamed for our economic ills. It's always easier to blame the weakest link in the society. I don't condone the crimes that are committed by those trying to get by, or anyone for that matter but we need to look harder at the corporations that steal big-time, pork barrel politics etc. They steal more from the taxpayer than any poor people ever could. Access to a good education is the answer—not just education to get a job but education that helps people think outside of the so called "box."

Education is what is going to get you out of a hole, and even then it's no guarantee. But if you don't have it, your chances will absolutely diminish even more.

JD: Right.

SM: And I think right now that the drop-out rate of Latinos out of high school is alarming. That's the plight, lack of education on all levels.

JD: Okay, this is the last question—in your opinion what were the problems that Chicanas faced within the Chicano movement?

SM: (hesitating, laughing) I think the biggest problem

we faced was sexism. (Laughing). You know, when I became aware of it—because in the beginning I really wasn't –I was so gun-ho Chicano Movement—we now had a connection, there seemed to be unity. We were all fighting for the same thing—equality, parity or so I thought. But when I did become aware that no, it wasn't really about equality for the women it was hard emotionally. Much later, I read a lot of articles that were written by Chicanas about the sexism they encountered and their deep hurt and disappointment. So, I wasn't alone. And I think my response was *Chicana*. Yet, I didn't want to be exclusive, I wanted to be inclusive.

But I found and still find that it's hard for people to change. It's wasn't just the men. Many women felt women should "wait for equality until the men got it." Then there are those people who think change is taking over the king's throne. They want to have what the "king" has and get even. And that's human nature, too. And you know what, that's the kind of movies that sell. (Laughing) It's a cruel world, Jenny (laughing).

JD: (Laughing)
SM: So I guess all you can do is, hold on to your path, your integrity. Write about what you feel, do the work you love as much as you possibly can, the way you want it done as often as you can. Your integrity in the work that you do is all you <u>really</u> have. That's all you can take with you. You can't take anything else.

I do think there are changes. There have been gains but there have been losses. The struggle continues on different and in unexpected ways. You know, 100 years ago, women died by age 40 and mostly in childbirth and that was thought of as normal. Along with that women had no rights. Things do change, not by themselves but by committed and passionate people with the help of enlightened allies. *Chicana* is a testament to that. The changes are incremental. Never fast enough for those who see what is just. And, there are women out there, Chicanas, who work hard and long to bring about changes in every area that affects our families and communities in unjust ways. Many times, as history has shown, a high price is paid. I'm interested in depicting these women who resist.

APPENDIX D

INTERVIEW WITH MARGARITA COTA-CÁRDENAS
Puppet (1985)
Personal/Career Questions:

JD: What is your upbringing? Where were you raised? (With this question I am more or less interested in knowing how you got involved in writing)

MCC: As you know from my personal and professional "bioblurb," [see it attached at end of this interview] I was born just north of the U.S.-Mexican border in Heber, California in 1941. My father was born in Mexico, brought to the U.S. by his parents as a child. My mother is Nuevo Mexicana (born in New Mexico), came to California to work as a domestic. Both my parents worked in the agricultural fields before they married. My father later became a labor contractor and was a bail bondsman for a time. My first language was Spanish, as was theirs. I learned to read Spanish from Mexican comic books. My home became bilingual when my brother and I began attending (English only permitted) grammar school in Heber. We moved to the central San Joaquín Valley of California, where in high school I wrote a column for the school paper (in English, of course), studied Spanish grammar and was encouraged to write and to go to college by my English teacher. In fact, I was not allowed to work in the fields by my father, who insisted that we get an education. I wrote my first essays and stories in high school, but in English class. I didn't write my first poem until 1970, it was a love poem (to an Iraqi lover of the moment), and it was in Spanish. Why in Spanish, I don't know except that was how it wanted to come out, rhyming here and there and all that. The guy couldn't even read Spanish, but that's how I had it in my head as I was writing and working on the poem. I started college as a drama major, ended up with a Ph.D. in Latin American and Peninsular literature, and wrote my first poetry collection in 1975, in a flurry and whirlwind of sleepless nights. Several love poems, but it's a feminist collection of "antimyths and counterlegends." And so forth.

JD: How do you identify yourself (i.e. as a woman, as a Chicana)? Why?

MCC: Labels are interesting; I've been called everything from a "vendida" or sell-out, to a left-wing flaming liberal feminist (I'm flattered either way, because as Pat Mora says, I'm a Mexican to Americans and an American to Mexicans, etc.) It's hard being Chicana. I identify myself as Margarita, Maggie, and a couple of other family nicknames. I seldom give a F- what most people call me.

JD: Are you a religious person?

MCC: I'm a non-practicing Catholic since my early twenties. Brought up Catholic, kiss the Bishop's ring and all that. I'm fairly open-minded about all religions, but not about intolerance. I can't tolerate intolerance, how about that?

JD: What authors and/or literary critics' works have been influential to you?

MCC: Oh, lots. Dickens, T.S. Eliot, Joyce, Fuentes, Castellanos, Nellie Campobello, Tomás Rivera. However, Miguel Méndez, Eliana Rivero and Tey Diana Rebolledo especially personally encouraged me to become an author.

JD: What inspires you to write? How do you describe the way you write?

MCC: As I say in *Sanctuaries of the Heart*, my second

novella yet published, my writing comes in whirlwinds that whip me about until I come face to face with whatever I've been running from. Of course, a poem, a story (like Puppet's), can arise from a specific event or incident(s): as innocuous as a birthday greeting, as enraging as the murder of Puppet and the "mind control" practiced on women.

JD: Was there any certain part of your upbringing that has been most influential in your writing?

MCC: My first language, border Spanish. Plus the oral tradition of telling stories, chismes (gossip) and chistes (jokes). My father was great for playing with words, lots of puns. I just remember the sounds, the music, the talking; my creative work is much more to my liking in Spanish/bilingual.

JD: To someone who does not know all of your work, but is familiar with a few pieces, how would you describe it? Is a common theme present in all your work?

MCC: My poetry is an easier "read" than my narratives, which tend to be "in your face" as far as technique and language. I guess common themes are relationships and community: love, family and "don't mess with me(us)." I don't write "safe" books. Each of the published books, and each poem, has its own voice and register. I address personal and community issues, sometimes the voices are militant or strident, sometimes ironic and humorous.

JD: Did you have a difficult time getting into the literary world being a woman of color?

MCC: I didn't ask anyone's permission to become "literary." We often independently publish, and as a consequence, distribution and acquiring a readership is very difficult. "Women of color" do not necessarily at present have a difficult time getting published, if they write popular genres, in English, and have chingona (aggressive or successful) agents.

JD: Is sexuality an important theme to you?
MCC: Well, we are all sexual beings, so why not rejoice in it? Actually, while there is eroticism and sensuality in my poetry especially, there are many themes: sociopolitical, criticism of the repression and subjugation of women; proscription of Chicanas, etc. Check out "Símbolo," which addresses "penis envy" in a bawdy, raucous voice; and no, Chicana feminists do not envy men's penises.

Questions about *Puppet*:

JD: When you wrote *Puppet*, what was your ultimate goal? What did you want to accomplish/portray with/by it? Why did you want to write/publish this book?
MCC: Petra Leyva, a graduate student in the fictional Southwest City, comes to terms with her own conscience as she sets about to learn the true circumstances of the police shooting of Puppet, a young Chicano laborer. The narrative zig-zags between past and present, creating a challenge for the uninitiated reader. I wanted to capture Chicano/Chicana reality, and its innumerable challenges.

JD: Did you consciously write the novella for the benefit of Chican@s? Did you write the novella specifically for women?
MCC: I write to exorcise myself. In my poetry as well as in my novels, I deal with being "triply colonized," as Mirandé calls it in *La Chicana: The Mexican American Woman:* the Chicana is a woman (a minority), part of an ethnic minority (Chicana/Latina/Mexicana etc.), and within her own minority culture, is subjected to *Machismo*. I think his definition sums it up, except that I also address gay/

lesbian issues in my more recent works.

JD: I have included *Puppet* as a part of the Chicana works I am studying—I classify these works as works by, about and for Chicanas[12385]—would you agree? That is, who was your target audience?

MCC: I initially wanted to tell Puppet's story, but through Petra Leyva's voice was drawn into exploring her own past, present and future in relation to her community and the dominant society. The "ideal reader" of the first edition, written mostly in Spanish, is probably a bilingual/bicultural Chicana; however, any bilingual/bicultural reader who is willing to read about being Chican@ in regard to issues of race, class and gender, might enjoy—and probably be challenged—by the reading of the book.

JD: Do you believe the target audience has changed since *Puppet* was written and published?

MCC: Well, the English translation now gives the novel an entire new circulation. As you know, it is being read abroad in the English/bilingual version by University of New Mexico Press; translated by Barbara Riess and Trino Sandoval with my collaboration (the book has a critical introduction by Tey Diana Rebolledo which analyzes the book's evolution and place in Chican@ literature since its first edition in 1985 with a small press).

JD: Viewing the *Puppet* today, 19 years after its debut (and 4 years after its bilingual version), is there anything you would change about it to bring it up to speed?

MCC: No. I wrote new poems, a second novella, and have started a third novel to bring myself "up to speed."

JD: Do you believe that through books like *Puppet* that offer insight into another's culture and traditions, the U.S. society will be more accepting of each other?

MCC: Judging from the success of many Latina and Chicana writers and artists, I would hope so. I hope our books and films are bringing about change. However, bigotry and racism in society, culture, and the arts still exist in spite of the popular achievements of African-American artists and writers for example. So the struggle is still on as far as I'm concerned.

JD: Do you know where the book has primarily been read (i.e. college classrooms)? Why do you think this is so?

MCC: The original Spanish/bilingual 1985 edition is still circulating "underground" and from hand to hand, recommended here and there. I think my books have been under-promoted by the publishers, although Juan Rodríguez (Relámpago Books) did a great job in the 80s. Also, as I said, my books are not "safe" nor easy to read: controversial? Too experimental? Who knows? I'm now retired and working on manuscripts and how to overcome distribution and publicity issues.

JD: Does the *Puppet* still apply today? Why? Or why not?

MCC: On the most primary thematic level, unfortunately yes. There is still the problem of either police brutality or police cover-ups in the community. If you read the book, you see it still applies regarding themes of race, class, gender.

JD: The book is subtitled, *Una novella chicana*. Why did you choose to subtitle it like this?

MCC: I wanted to emphasize the nature of the subject: about Chican@ reality, a short novella, and a possible play on the combination of "nov-ella" (a new novel by a 'she').

JD: When we were e-mailing about *Puppet* a year ago, you said that you have had students from Europe contact you about the work—why do you think this is? Why is Chicana literature becoming popular in Europe?

MCC: I think the publication in 2000 of the English translation (along with the Spanish) has sent *Puppet* and word of my work because of the introduction by Dr. Rebolledo, into a widening readership of literature by Latinas/Chicanas/Hispanics in Europe. Much of this growing interest is fomented by the fact that Chicana writers are being studied abroad in many Departments of Philology and Linguistics, where English (and literature in English) is studied. These students then write papers often; they and their professors present papers on a respective author, poet, film, etc. It's an intriguing development. Chicano literature has been studied abroad, such as in Germany, since its inception in the "Chicano Renaissance" of the 60s anyway, since many of those writers either wrote mostly in English or were translated early on. As you know, Chicana writers however, do not experience the attention of anthologists nor critics, nor do they begin to gain attention at literary venues until the mid to late 70s.

JD: For the purposes of my research, I am not as focused on the purpose of *Puppet*, that is to tell the story of what happened to Tony López as much as I am interested in the commonalities between your writing and the other writers I look at. Is that disappointing to you?

MCC: If you read the book, you got the message about Puppet's dilemma and tragic end. It is not, as I said above, an isolated incident. As to literary criticism or classroom study, there have been a number of papers presented at conferences on *Puppet* and my poetry, including articles that cite my work, especially in the last two decades. Papers or articles on *Puppet* have focused on many facets;

one of the most common mentions is the use of language. I guess you could "Google" to see the cites, however modest, on my work. I'm grateful for any reader that takes on Puppet to read. Each reader sees what he sees, and something may "speak" to her in particular. That's my hope.

JD: Why did you want to publish a bilingual version?

MCC: Because I was told there was a need for *Puppet* in English, by students and professors alike, and because "Memo" can't read Spanish, and I wanted him to have a copy of the story he had inspired that he could read. ("Memo" was Puppet's boss in the story.)

JD: Why did you write this book in Spanish originally?

MCC: Because I had to. And it's actually "bilingual" because it has some English in it; just like we talk in real life in this part of the world.

JD: Can you tell me a little bit more about your re-writing of La Malinche's myth in the chapter, "Discurso de la Malinche"?

MCC: I first wrote this chapter in 1982, while writing *Puppet*. I presented the section "Discurso de la Malinche" at the National Association of Chicana/Chicano Studies at Arizona State University that Spring, on a panel on Chicana literature. What can I tell you, except that it's another example of my "anti-myths and counter-legends" *onda* ('groove'). And Marina, or Malintzin Tenepal, the historical figure that Chicana writers especially have sought to redeem from the cultural stigma of "traitress," would be my main role model. Other archetypes that have inspired Chicanas and other women writers and scholars as well as artists, have been Sor Juana Inés, and the revisioned Virgen de Guadalupe (think of Alma López' renderings of contemporary Guadalupes).

JD: Do you think *Puppet* would make a good film (I've thought it would because of all the flashbacks)?

MCC: I've been told many times it would make a good play, a good movie, etc. Funny, too, because when I first showed the core draft (five-six pages) of Puppet's life and death to my then Chicano Lit. professor, Dr. Miguel Méndez (the renown Chicano writer), he told me "Tiene mucha garra!" ("It really grabbed the reader!") We thought it might make a good TV script, but I was working on my doctorate; I started working on the novel, in earnest, in 1981, when I came to Arizona State to teach. Anyway, we do have plans for a screenplay or play.

JD: What sort of response did you get after *Puppet* came out in 1985? How about 2000?

MCC: Slow, but very good response. For young readers not used to contemporary fiction techniques, however, it can be formidable to read even the English. However, if you can follow García Márquez, Carlos Fuentes, Isabel Allende in translation, and of course, the biggies in English such as James Joyce, Faulkner, Pynchon, etc., then *Puppet* may be a good read for you.

JD: What is the meaning of "ARGO"? (I know you mean ALGO, but can you explain the repetition of the word in the novella, please?)

MCC: "ALGO" or "argo," as Puppet pronounced the word, "something" is used to remind the reader of the association made of Puppet with Hamlet, in the funeral parlor. "Something," according to *Puppet*, as with *Hamlet*, smells "fishy" in Southwest City, and Puppet reminds Petra (her conscience, sub-conscience) that "something" needs to be ferreted out.

JD: María, Petra's daughter, in the novella is very interested in her bicultural reality as well as the Chicano

Movement, César Chávez, the March of Delano, etc. Did you purposely include María's character to discuss or bring up the Chican@ Movements?

MCC: Yes; she is the prototype of the young Chicana student-activist, a foil to pique Petra's indecision to continue forward with the investigation of Puppet's death, writing about it, make a personal, social and political commitment, etc. It also reminds Petra about her own dark secret: she had not supported the March in 1965. I had a similar experience, but have been a long-time supporter of the United Farm Workers. In fact, that same campus developed one of the first Chicano Studies Programs in California in the late 60s; I was one of the members of that committee. I have since been involved, especially through my writing and teaching, in helping students and the community at large, become aware of Chican@ history, culture and civilization. I have belonged to the National Association of Chicana/Chicano Studies, and for many years, to the Modern Languages Association, and for five years, a member of the Chicano Literature Committee. No formal organization makes you part of the "Movement." You just do your part to help in the struggle for peace, love, justice, and that's what María in *Puppet* represents. Of course, this entire interview represents my personal opinions.

General Chican@ Questions:

JD: What is the current plight of the Chicana in your opinion?

MCC: You'd think we would no longer have a "plight," after all this time, wouldn't you? In works like Rebolledo and Rivero's *Infinite Divisions*, and Cherríe Moraga and Gloria Anzaldúa's groundbreaking politicizing texts, the problem is evident: we no longer have to walk behind the Macho, but he really can't tolerate our striding ahead. Just talk to Chicana academics and Chicana/Latina writers, and they'll have stories that will enlighten you. We have internationally recognized writers like Cisneros, and Chicana literature is studied all over in English departments, Women's Studies, Spanish departments, Chicana/Chicano studies, etc. Yet we still have to fight with our own male colleagues to gain respect and recognition, especially the "old guard." The gay or lesbian artists still need our support, along with our other sisters, in gaining (and keeping) academic posts so that the word keeps on going. I embrace being a woman; my life is an open book, and I write when I feel I just can't stand it any longer. It's a release and a liberation. And that's what I want for us all: Liberation. I wish for our children, an end to terrorism and the politics of vengeance; and "just say no" to religious fanaticism.

"Bioblurb"
(Used with permission from Margarita Cota-Cárdenas)

Margarita Cota-Cárdenas was born in 1941 in the rural town of Heber, Imperial County, California, just eight miles north of the Mexico-U.S. border. She spoke only Spanish before starting first grade, and her home became increasingly bilingual through the years. Her family became involved in agricultural or farm labor from their early years in the U.S., and after their migration over several years to the central San Joaquín Valley in California, they settled there. It was in the San Joaquín Valley that Margarita graduated from high school in Newman, California; from college in Turlock, California; and earned a Master's degree from University of California, Davis, in 1968. After returning to teach two years at her alma mater in Turlock, she came to the University of Arizona to pursue her doctoral degree, which she received in 1980. She raised three children during these years. Except for 1980-1981, Margarita has lived in Arizona from 1970 to the present. She taught at Arizona State University for over twenty years until Fall 2002, when she retired as Professor Emerita. She principally taught bilingual Spanish, Chicano/Chicana literature and Mexican literature courses.

Margarita has written since high school, where she wrote a column called "Just Talking." She has published short stories, which have in part been incorporated in her novels, *Puppet* (1985), and *Sanctuaries* (2005). *Puppet*, considered to be the first novel in Spanish by a Chicana in the U.S., was translated into English by Dr. Trino Sandoval of Phoenix College and Dr. Barbara Riess of Allegheny College, with the author and was published in a bilingual edition by The University of New Mexico Press in 2000. She also is the cofounder of Scorpion Press, which in the 1970s published four books of poetry, including her first collection *Noches despertando inConciencias*. Her second collection, *Marchitas de mayo: sones pa'al pueblo*, appeared in 1989.

She has been inspired by writers like Tomás Rivera, to "write about what you know, what has happened to you or to people you know." Rivera maintained that sincerity and good writing went hand in hand, rather than dogma, in describing the Chicano/Chicana experience. Margarita says: "You need to have those ganas, a sense of humor, and a lot of *persistence*, to make it in this life!"

APPENDIX E

INTERVIEW WITH SUSANA BLAUSTEIN MUÑOZ
La Ofrenda: The Days of the Dead (1988)
Personal/Career Questions:

JD: What is your upbringing?
SBM: I was born in Argentina in a Latino-Jewish family. When I was eighteen I left home for Israel where I got a degree in Fine Arts (painting and photography). Later I moved to the U.S.A. where I studied filmmaking in San Francisco. My second film *Las Madres* was nominated for an Academy Award.

JD: Does anyone in your family write or tell stories? (I am interested in knowing how you were encouraged to make films that tell stories).
SBM: No one in my family writes or tells stories. My father was fond of photography. He died very young and *La Ofrenda: The Days of the Dead* was to honor his memory.

JD: How did you end up in the United States making films?
SBM: To make a long story shot, I moved to San Francisco in 1979 where I studied filmmaking at the San Francisco Art Institute.

JD: What are your thoughts about feminism?
SBM: To begin with I am a feminist. I believe in the power of women to change the patterns of the mostly patriarchal society. I believe feminism helps women to

come out of the closet and be themselves.

JD: How did the Feminist Movement influence your filmmaking or were you already consciente of the power of women?
SBM: The Feminist Movement was an important stimulus to my inner feeling about its principles.

JD: Growing up did you have a role model?
SBM: My fine arts teacher in high school was someone I looked up to for support. She opened the door for me to understand and value the fine arts.

JD: How do you identify yourself? Why?
SBM: I identify myself as a Latino-Jewish filmmaker. I am also an open-minded lesbian out of the closet.

JD: What filmmakers/directors and/or film critics have been influential to you? How come?
SBM: I love Woody Allen. I feel he is a versatile director.

JD: To someone who does not know all of your work, but is familiar with a few pieces, how would you describe it? Is a common theme present in all your work?
SBM: My work has a common theme which is looking for social justice. It is difficult to stand by one's principles, in a world dominated by men.

JD: What inspires you to make films? How do you describe the way you make films?
SBM: I am mainly a visual person. I went from photography into filmmaking. When I am making a film, I trust my gut feeling.

JD: Are you a religious person?
SBM: I am an agnostic Jew.

Latina Filmakers & Writers

JD: What effects did the church and/or your family have on you growing up?

SBM: My parents helped me in spite of their different point of view. My parents believed in having a liberal profession.

JD: Was there any certain part of your upbringing that has been most influential in your filmmaking?

SBM: My father used to make super-eight films.

JD: Did you have a difficult time getting into the film world being a woman of color?

SBM: I don't think that being a woman of color had any effect in getting into the film world.

JD: Is sexuality an important theme in Chican@ film and/or in your films?

SBM: I dealt with sexuality in my first film. It was a film about coming out of the closet as a Latino lesbian.

JD: Is the Chicano relationship to the dominant culture something you like to explore in your filmmaking?

SBM: I believe I dealt with the Chicano relationship to the dominant culture in my film *La Ofrenda*.

Questions about *La Ofrenda: The Days of the Dead*:

JD: Why the two language title?
SBM: I believe in bilingual education.

JD: Did you consciously make the film for the benefit of Chican@s?

SBM: I made the film as a tribute to my father; he died very young.

JD: When you made *La Ofrenda*, what was your ultimate goal? What did you want to accomplish/portray with it?
SBM: My ultimate goal was to share with the audience a bi-cultural experience.

JD: In the film there is a transition from Oaxaca to San Francisco, is this transition meant to bring attention to the link between Mexican and Chicano communities?
SBM: Yes, the film is meant to bring attention to the link between Mexican and Chicano communities.

JD: What is the current plight of the Chicana in your opinion? Do you believe it has changed since *La Ofrenda* was made?
SBM: I believe that the current plight of the Chicana today is to keep on fighting against discrimination, by the mainly white society.

JD: As I discovered, the flyer for the film said, the film was the "Chicana's quest to understand her culture". Why is this?
SBM: No comment!

JD: Did you choose to make this film specifically for women? That is, who was your target audience?
SBM: The film was not made specifically for women; my target audience was primarily the PBS audience.

JD: Viewing the film today, 16 years after its debut, is there anything you would change about it to bring it up to speed? Or does the film still apply today? Why? Or why not?
SBM: I think the film still applies today.

JD: Do you believe that through films like *La Ofrenda* that offer insight into another's culture and traditions, the U.S. society will be more accepting of each other?

SBM: I believe that films like *La Ofrenda* can help to bridge the gap between Latino and white society.

JD: Is *La Ofrenda* an indictment against Mexican culture and Anglo culture? That is, against Mexican culture for its lack of acceptance of homosexuality and against Anglo culture for its ignorance toward other cultures?

SBM: *La Ofrenda* is an indictment against Anglo culture for its ignorance towards other cultures.

JD: Do you know where the film has primarily been shown (i.e. College classrooms, Fine Arts Theatres)? Why do you think this is so?

SBM: *La Ofrenda* is distributed by direct cinema, a distribution company out of Los Angeles. They have a network of schools, universities, churches and other cultural places. It has been shown in several countries (both in Europe and Latin America).

JD: I have included *La Ofrenda: The Days of the Dead* as a part of the Chicana works I am studying—I classify these works as works by, about and for Chicanas[12386]—would you agree?

SBM: *La Ofrenda* is a work by Chicanas with the intention to reach a wide audience.

JD: Additionally, I am including my discussion of *La Ofrenda: The Days of the Dead* with two other films and three other books. I claim that *La Ofrenda: The Days of the Dead* as well as the other two films and three books are examples of Chicanisma, or the concept of "sisterhood", that is Chicana artists that give Chicanas a name, a voice and an image. Would you agree? Why or why not?

SBM: I agree with you in the concept of "sisterhood", that is Chicana artists that give Chicanas a name, a voice and an image.

JD: As part of your self-identification, from what point of view were you coming from when you made *La Ofrenda*?

SBM: As I explained earlier *La Ofrenda* is a tribute to the memory of my father.

JD: Was there anything that was said (either by critics, acquaintances and/or friends) about *La Ofrenda* when it first came out that really bothered you? For example, did anyone misinterpret a message in the film?

SBM: No comments!

JD: What sort of response did you get after *La Ofrenda* came out in 1988?

SBM: There was a wide response for *La Ofrenda*, primarily by high school teachers (teachers for bilingual education).

JD: Are you surprised that someone, i.e. me, if still interested in your film 16 years later?

SBM: No, I am not surprised that you are interested in my film 16 years later. My film is still appealing nowadays.

JD: How come you made this film with Lourdes Portillo? That is, how did you end up making this film with Ms. Portillo?

SBM: After the success of *Las Madres: The Mothers of Plaza de Mayo*, which we also made together, we decided to make *La Ofrenda*.

General Chican@ Questions:

JD: Were you at all involved in the Chicano or Chicana Movements?

SBM: No, I was not involved in the Chicano/Chicana Movements.

JD: Do you think Chicanas have progressed since the 1970s, that is, since the beginning of the Chicana Movement?

SBM: I believe that Chicanas have progressed a lot since the 1970s. The Chicana Movement is still alive and kicking.

JD: Do you think it will ever die?

SBM: As long as there are Chicanos and Chicanas, the Movement will never die.

APPENDIX F

INTERVIEW WITH LOURDES PORTILLO
La Ofrenda: The Days of the Dead (1988)
Personal/Career Questions:

JD: What's your upbringing? Where did you come from? Basically, what I want to know is how did you get to the point where you wanted to make films?
LP: Well, I was born in Mexico. When I was 13 years old, the whole family immigrated to Los Angeles. We were in Los Angeles, and since it's like a film company town, there's a lot of filmmaking going on. Eventually, when I was around 20 years old I was invited to work in educational film. And in working in that film, I realized that I was searching to find out what it was that I wanted to do with my life at age twenty. So, I didn't know what it was, but when I worked on the film, I felt like I understood how films were made, and I liked what I saw and I liked what I did—so I started pursuing that. And then there was like a process, a formative process of working and learning. But that was the initial impetus at age 21.

JD: Well, that's good. You figured out before I did, and I'm 25.
LP: I know it's not easy, I've seen my children go through that.

JD: So, does anyone in your family write or tell stories, I mean, I have noticed that your films are about telling a story.
LP: No, but I come from kind of a tradition of everyone. Really, my parents always told stories, they always talked

about their life in Mexico. They were always very amusing actually, or tragic or whatever, they were always fun to listen to.

JD: That's neat; stories are something that isn't really told anymore—too much television watching.
LP: I think so.

JD: Switching subjects, what are your thoughts about feminism and are you a feminist?
LP: Yeah, of course, I am a feminist. I believe that women should have equal ranking in the world in every way and of course, we're way behind. And I do everything I can to put us at that equal footing, so I am a feminist. I don't know what else to tell you, I am not an orthodox feminist. I mean, I did come from that time, but I think feminism has changed. Younger people are different types of feminists; even men are feminists which is so wonderful.
JD: Yes, I agree.
LP: That's beautiful to watch. I mean to see my kids be feminists and they're boys, I thought, "My god," this is like better than I thought.
JD: Makes the world a better place.

JD: Was the feminist movement, per se, in the 1970s influential for your filmmaking?
LP: Not really. I can't say that. I think that I must have been influenced in some way, but I think what influenced me more than feminism was all the upheavals in Latin America—the human rights' struggles, the struggles for democracy, that sort of thing was very influential in my life. Even more than feminism, feminism was always there because I was experiencing it first hand in the US, but I think that my work is more influenced by Latin American life.

JD: Okay.

JD: How do you identify yourself?
LP: I would say I am a Mexican first because I was born in Mexico, and I'm very attached, those were my formative years. A lot of my language comes from there, my philosophy; my interest in life, my interest in drama, my interest in almost everything comes from that early age. So, I am very Mexican. In coming to the United States I feel like I have to have another experience that was not of being honored as a Mexican. In fact, I was marginalized as a Chicana so I am a Mexican with a Chicana experience—a politicized stance on this immigrant life, really.
JD: That's unfortunate, but seems to be the pattern.
LP: Yeah.

JD: What languages did you speak growing up? I mean, you spoke Spanish until you were 13, or did you have any English influence until then?
LP: Yeah, I spoke some English when I was younger because I went to school, and you learn it in school, so I did speak some English when I came here, but I mostly spoke Spanish, and I've kept it up. I've been speaking Spanish all of my life, I try to learn other languages as well. I think it is a key to understanding other cultures. You start understanding the culture, and you start understanding other ways of being which is so enriching.

JD: Growing up did you have a role model?
LP: I have been asked this several times, and I cannot tell you that I did because I spent so much time struggling that I just felt like I was always in constant struggle to get done what I needed to get done that I didn't have a chance to sort of mediate on whether or not I was imitating anyone or not. But later on, I came to admire a number of different people for their strength and their ability to

express themselves. But I don't think that growing up I had a model. I mean, maybe people in my family, my father, my uncle, my aunt, people like that.
JD: Right.

JD: So more along those lines, when you got into filmmaking at 21, were there, and this is a typical interview question—
LP: Don't worry...

JD: Were there filmmakers/directors/film critics that were influential to you?
LP: When I started getting into it at the very very beginning I wasn't thinking so much about filmmakers and directors and all that, it seemed to me to be something more like a trade. It was something you learned, which in fact it is, and it has become totally romanticized. So it was more like a trade, but as I started learning more and more about films, then I started distinguishing a good film from a bad film and what it was saying and all that. There were so many filmmakers at that time in the 70s that were like really admirable like Buñuel, and Fellini, all these people that were extraordinary talented and I don't think it has been repeated since. I admire them very very much.

JD: Do you think that there is common theme in your films?
LP: Yeah, I think people end up making the same films over and over again.

JD: (Laughing) Really?
LP: I think so; I think there are a lot of common themes. I mean, I don't think there is one, I think there are several. There are many. It seems like I am making that film over and over again, it has to do a lot of time with Latin American culture, the complexity of that culture, it has to

do with human rights, it has to do with family, intrigue, mystery, and those kinds of things really kind of capture my imagination. So, I have used them in different combinations.

JD: I agree from the films I have seen of yours. But, I mean, they are all unique, I wouldn't say they were all the same.
LP: No, no of course, not. But they have kind of the same root, the same interest.

JD: So more along the lines of what inspires to make films, for example, for *La Ofrenda*, what was it that you're like, "I want to make a film about the day of the dead."
LP: Oh, well, you see this is what happens when you start making films—you react to them—against them or whatever—what happened was after doing *Las Madres: La plaza de mayo*, it was so painful to make that film—to see all the suffering that people had gone through that I felt I wanted to make a joyous film about death. And then I immediately thought about Mexico and how Mexicans view death and its roots and ancient Indian culture. So, it was a reaction to *Las Madres* in a way, and at the same time it was a reaffirmation of my own culture.

JD: Okay. It's so neat to talk to you because things start making sense to me...do you consider yourself a religious person?
LP: NO, well, not in the typical way I think I do believe in religiosity towards nature, I guess, towards our sacredness of our lives and how we spend them and how we use our lives and how we use our voices. I believe all that, but I am not a very traditional religious person. I like Buddhism a lot because it holds you accountable—you have to account for every action that you make, and if it's a bad, then bad will come from it. And if it is good, it just

creates more good. You know that kind of religion I like.

JD: So growing up in Mexico up until the age of 13, were you influenced at all by the Catholic Church, as a woman did that effect you? Or even now being considered a Chicana, is that an issue?

LP: No, not really. I feel like that my life was permeated by this religious atmosphere that one lives in Mexico, but I think it was a little bit removed from my daily experience. I didn't feel any deep feeling of religiosity. So I was always a little bit marginal. All my life, I think, I felt like I was taking a different stand. No, I guess against it or for it, sometimes. It wasn't like I was following a strict path...

JD: Right...did you have a difficult time, after the age of 21 when you figured out that you wanted to do films, getting into the film world? Being, as you said, coming to this country, being an immigrant or having that status?

LP: Absolutely, I lived in a very racist place, which is Los Angeles, and I wanted to make films which were really a very expensive proposition. Making a film even in those days, I mean now I could see that kids could start making films digitally, but at that time it was so expensive and also there had been a very long tradition of portraying America as this single race place that was not interested in the voices of colored people. So there was no way, I knew there was no way; I could see my limitations that I could get to make big films. There was no possibility, I wasn't rich, I was willing to do it, but I knew I couldn't do it. So my first job was for a documentary, and I realized that it is very different. It is not as romanticized as narrative filmmaking, so I started focusing on that, so I thought that was a good way for me to start and in fact I liked it so much that I stayed there. I have also made narrative films; I am still into the narrative films. But in Los Angeles at that point and in that time, it was impossible for me to even dream of making narrative films.

JD: Right...so, okay, you mentioned that when you came to the U.S. and still today, that there is the idea of a one race society...so do you think you try to explore that in your films, the Chicano/Chicana relationship to that one race society?
LP: Yes, definitely, I felt like it was really important especially because there were so many of us. For us to put our lives out there and to focus on who we are and how we are just as human beings, not as stereotypes, and it was very very important and that was like a mission for me to be able to that.

JD: Yeah, I am glad you did.
LP: Thank you.

JD: I am going to move on to questions about *La Ofrenda*. But, is there anything else you'd like to add?
LP: No, that's fine. If you think of something, you tell me.
JD: I will. I am full of questions, always.

Questions about *La Ofrenda*:

JD: Why the two language title—why *La Ofrenda* and then *The Days of the Dead*?
LP: It was again the reaffirmation of being in this country and being bilingual and reaffirming the fact that we're here. And that's what I did with most of my films.

JD: I know that you have mentioned that you had several goals with it... but did you consciously make the film for the benefit of Chicanos and Chicanas?
LP: You now, not really, I mean, I do, because I think

that will come naturally, but I also make films of everybody. I'd prefer my films to speak to everyone; it is also an invitation to understand us. In another away, I can say it is a two fold kind of purpose. To kind of present ourselves and say this is who we are.

JD: So more along those lines...in the film where there is the transition between Oaxaca and San Francisco, is that to show the link between Mexicanos and Chicanos?

LP: Yes, yeah, that we've come here, and we continue the tradition although it has been transformed in some way.

JD: The flyer of the film said that the film is "a Chicana's quest to understand her culture" was that something you came up with or...?

LP: No...I think somebody must have written that. Maybe it seems that way to some people.

JD: Did you choose to make this film, specifically, I know you say for all audiences, but do you think it focuses on women at all?

LP: I think it focuses on women as carriers of cultures, that women are the ones that retain culture but not in a very conscious way just by making food, by serving food, by collecting food, that sort of thing. Women are the living culture, I believe that.

JD: So when you make a film—do you think of a target audience? You had mentioned, of course that you would like everyone to see it. Yet, do you kind of have an idea in mind of what will happen to it? *La Ofrenda*, for example?

LP: That film was used a lot for educational purposes, and I think that's what its intention was too. Because in those days the Days of the Dead were hardly celebrated. Yes, it depends on the film.

JD: What is the current plight of the Chicana in your opinion? And do you believe that it has changed since *La Ofrenda* was made?

LP: I think that Chicana culture has advanced considerably. Like during the whole Civil Rights struggle, a lot of Chicanos went to college, a lot of Chicanos have been really well educated and have gone into positions of influence that have helped other Chicanos. So, I think that it is really, in one way it has been wonderful, and in another way we have so many immigrants, and we have so many people that are still suffering a lot of economic deprivation and a lot of racism all around the country, a lot of bad things—but there's some good and there's some bad. I think that as along that Mexicans look to the deeper values of our culture, I think that things will get better. As long as we don't adapt the culture of consumerism, and this voracity for money everything will be okay.

JD: Yes, I agree. Viewing the film today, 16 years later, is there anything that you would change about it to bring it up to today's speed? Or do you think it still applies today?

LP: I think it still kind of applies today—it is not up-to-date in terms of the San Francisco thing, but I would just make it a little bit shorter.

JD: Really? What would you cut?

LP: I don't know, I am not sure, but I just think it needs a few minutes off—this is just as a filmmaker.

JD: Do you think that films like *La Ofrenda* offer insight into another's culture and traditions and that because of this, and you have said this already in one way or another, you think society would be more accepting of one another? How you address the white Americans that are visiting Mexico, and that whole issue; can you kind of expand on that, please?

LP: Well, it was just interesting how there was this difference in understanding of death—it was like a clash of cultures. You're looking at life and death this way, and this ancient culture is looking at this other way—I think that now perhaps there could be a bridge between those two. I think there is more of an understanding of Mexican culture now. It was just fortuitous that those people [the white tourists] were there at that point. And I asked them, and that's what they came up with—and some people have reacted negatively towards that and said, "Well, how could you?"

JD: Yes.

LP: But I guess at that point, I could.

JD: Yes, I thought it was a great contrast, so I didn't have a problem with it.

LP: Oh, that's good.

JD: Do you know where the film has primarily been shown and this kind of goes back to what we were talking about earlier—

LP: Yeah, I think it has been shown a lot in schools, universities and libraries. I think this film has actually had the widest distribution of any of my films in the U.S.

JD: Okay, well, that's neat.

LP: Yeah, it is. I think it has helped look at Mexican culture differently, so I think it's great.

JD: On the lines of sexuality, you address homosexuality in the film; can you expand a little bit more on that, why you address it and that sort of thing?

LP: Oh, because I think that was a tradition in that place that the transvestites had a moment of dressing up and being accepted whereas in any other moment they would be transgressive and open for attack, really. So that was kind of my point.

JD: Okay...What sort of response did you get when it came out in '88?
LP: I had just finished *Las Madres* which was a very hard-hitting political film that had a lot of success and this seemed kind of soft to people. But then after awhile people kind of caught on to what it was about, it took a little time and then there was a great demand of the film because it opened up doors for different people, it opened up understanding.

JD: Right, so was there anything that was said about the film that bothered you? As far as kind of offended you?
LP: No, not really. I think only one time I was attacked a Flaherty seminar by some photographer saying that the images are just as prevalent in American culture as in Mexican culture. And I was just saying that we're looking at it in different ways—death here is something that is gory and horrible, and in Mexico it was different, a different way of looking at it. But that was the only thing.

JD: And you had said that some people were offended by the whole American interview part in Mexico. But that didn't necessarily bother you?
LP: No, no it didn't because I know that at that moment in time if I would have gone out anywhere else a lot of people would have said that.

JD: Right.
LP: Americans are very sensitive sometimes as how they are portrayed they don't see themselves as how they are. And I think it is important to be able to look at other people's perspective of one.

JD: Yes, I agree...I've included *La Ofrenda*, and I think you might have gathered this from what I have sent you already, but as a part of the Chicano works that I am studying, and I classify these works for, by and about Chicanas which actually Rosa Linda Fregoso, who you've worked with a lot, talked about in her book, *The Bronze Screen*. Would you believe that *La Ofrenda* is a film that is for, by and about Chicanas, but not limited to Chicanas?

LP: Limited to, right. Yeah, I totally agree. Because I think we live in this culture, so I believe we have to speak to all of that. That's our obligation as artists.

JD: Another kind of thesis that I have for my work is along the lines of the concept of sisterhood—all the works I am studying some how address, what you just said, the relationship between Chicanos and Anglo culture...trying to bring about an awareness that there are other cultures in the U.S. besides the European American one.

LP: Well, I think that all of us can serve as an example for the rest of us, that we are living in a multicultural society, and we have many really different interesting cultures, it is not a mono- or bi-cultural world that we can represent ourselves in art in all these multiple and that we can speak to the humanity that is common amongst us. That is the most important thing that we can do—to stress the human aspects, what are commonalities, and that way bring about more understanding and cohesion instead of division. So, I do believe, firmly believe it, and I think my work talks about that in many different ways.

JD: Yes.

JD: How much did La Ofrenda cost to make? How were you able to make it (i.e. get equipment, find a crew, etc.)?

LP: We made it with grant form the organizations listed in the credits. I don't remember exactly how much it cost without having to do hours of investigation.

JD: Have you worked on La Ofrenda since?
LP: I have not touched it.

JD: How did you end up making the film with Susana Muñoz? I know you made *Las Madres* together, but how come you wanted to make another film together?
LP: We decided to continue our work together but Susana left the project after the principal shooting of it, so I did the post-production.

General Chican@ Movement Questions:

JD: Were you at involved in the Chicano Movement?
LP: I was a little bit too old for the Chicano Movement. I was neither here nor there, but my brothers and sisters were very very active in the Chicano movement. I was actually tending to my little babies at that point, so I didn't have time. But I could see it through their experience, what they were going through, what their struggles were, and I felt very sympathetic and I was always listening, trying to comprehend and trying to change the world in the minimal way that I could, but later on when I had more time of course it was in making films. I didn't specifically take part in marches and stuff like that, but, I mean, my brothers and sisters did.
JD: Ok.

JD: So, although you weren't directly involved, what was it like being considered a Chicana in those years? I mean were you—
LP: Was I offended?

JD: Not offended, but more so, how were you treated by society?
LP: Like a Mexican, of course! You know, in a terrible way, it was not nice. I mean, the Chicano Movement

offered us an option of being more defiant and of being more aggressive instead of taking all of that abuse. So it was a really good thing.

JD: Okay...you touched on this earlier, but I wanted to ask you again to see if you'll expand on it—do you think Chicanas have progressed since the 1970s, kind of since the Chicana Movement which was after the Chicano Movement?

LP: Yes and no, I am always torn between those two things I think some of us who have kept the values of that Movement alive have helped others, and I think, yes we have. And there are others that have not, and I think it all hinges on keeping our most noble values as human beings alive.

JD: Do you think that the Chicana Movement is still alive today?

LP: Yeah, alive and old.

JD: (Laughing) Why do you say that?

LP: No, I do think, of course, I think so. I think so. I don't know because I am a certain age, and I don't know exactly how it is in the universities now, but I have a tendency to think that they are just equally active and more intelligent, they have had better education—everything is much better now in that way for the women I think.

JD: What are you currently working on?

LP: Right now? I don't know I am a little bit in between things.

JD: Okay...I emailed you awhile ago to ask you if you knew of any way to help the women in Juarez, after I saw your film [*Senorita Extravida*].

LP: It is very hard for me. Did I tell you to get in touch

with Amigos por Juarez?

JD: NO.

LP: Okay, I think they are the best group and that's in El Paso.

JD: Well, I am finished; unless you have something else you'd like to add?

LP: No, I think that you did it.

JD: Good. Well, I really appreciate your time, and I thank you very much.

LP: Oh, you're welcome and thank you for taking the time to do this I really appreciate it and everybody else does too.

APPENDIX G

INTERVIEW WITH ERLINDA GONZÁLES-BERRY
Paletitas de Guayaba (1991)
Personal/Career Questions:

JD: What is your upbringing? That is, how did you get to the point where you wanted to write a book?

EGB: I was brought up in a tightly knit family seeped in rural Nuevomexicano culture. This included the use of Spanish as the primary language of communication within the community, a shared sense of belonging to a specific space—Nuevo México—, of values and of cultural practices, including a blend of folk and official Catholicism. I never aspired to write a book. Writing just fell in line as part of my professional development as a college professor.

JD: How do you identify yourself ethnically? Why?

EGB: My primary core identity is Nuevomexicana. Within the social environment in which I was raised, this was definitely a distinct regional/cultural/ethnic category that was characterized in relation to two other cultural groups: Native American and Anglo. The cultural milieu that surrounded me had developed in a particular regional space over hundreds of years; therefore it was peculiar to that region. But it had its roots in Spanish (language, religion, folk practices) culture and indigenous Mexican culture (world view, folk practices, language, religion and much, much more). In Spanish, the ethnic label preferred by our community as I was growing up was *mexican@*. Later I became, and continue to be Chicana. Now that I find myself working with people whose roots go back to a variety of Latin American countries and with whom I identify on a number of levels, I also consider myself Latina. My ethnic identity hence is multiple, fluid and strategic.

JD: What are your thoughts about feminism?

EGB: Feminism of the white, middle class variety certainly had an impact on my life, as it was through it that I first came to question what it meant to be a woman. However, as I explored this brand of feminism, I soon came to see its shortcomings in addressing that part of me and women like me whose lives were deeply affected by class and racism. This led me to begin to explore what it meant to be a woman within my own cultural matrix and also to link feminism to other kinds of oppression. In other words, I found feminism by itself too limiting an ideology for grasping and addressing broader issues of social injustice and oppression.

JD: How did the Feminist Movement influence your writing or were you already consciente of the power of women?

EGB: My consciencia of the power of women was already present in that I was brought up among incredibly powerful mujeres. However, my theoretical understanding of gender construction was facilitated by feminist thinking and more importantly by the feminist thinking of Chicana and other women of color theorists. This consciencia certainly influenced my writing, in that it gave me freedom to speak as I saw fit.

JD: Are you a religious person? What effects did the church or your family have on you growing up? As a woman?

EGB: Catholicism was a central component of my upbringing. When I got to college, I began to experience a great deal of conflict between my religious beliefs and new ways of looking at the world and understanding my place within it. I was bothered that my religious beliefs got in my way of thinking for myself. I especially had problems with religious doctrine and my desire to develop as a thinking and desiring woman. I walked away from the church when I was 23, but in many ways, I think it still has a hold on me. My sense of spirituality has undoubtedly sprung from my early Catholic upbringing, but it is more and more rooted in the wonder and beauty of the natural world and all that it contains of the supernatural.

JD: What languages did you speak growing up? Which do you speak now?
EGB: I spoke Spanish and English. I had the opportunity to develop my Spanish through formal study at the university...I have studied French and Portuguese but am not fluent in either.

JD: Growing up, did you have a role model? How about now, do you have a heroine, someone you admire?
EGB: I had many role models growing up. Abuelas and tías were powerful figures who taught me to work, to be sentimental and dramatic, and to always open up a space for humor. But the most important role model was my mother. She came from a very poor family, yet managed to educate herself at a time when most women remained at home. She became a teacher at 17 and, in fact, was my teacher from grades 5-8. From her I learned that women could be both/and. They could fulfill their culturally defined role as wife and mother, yet become financially independent and exert agency in the public realm. She was an incredibly compassionate human being, but she could be tough as nails when she had to be. What most amazes me about this woman is that despite all the deprivation and limitations, she rose above it all and succeeded in giving her five daughters a strong sense of personal worth.

And though she is gone, I continue to admire her and to hold her as my number one heroine. Other important role models were my modern dance teacher, Elizabeth Wells; she really opened up the world to me, and Tamara Holzapel, my mentor throughout graduate school. She taught me all about Latin America and its literature and also about the stuff necessary for surviving in a male-dominated profession.

JD: What inspires you to write? How do you describe the way you write?

EGB: What inspires me to write is the urge to tell a story. I grew up among great story tellers, who taught me to love shaping a world through language. However, my formal education made me a bit too analytical, and this tendency frequently gets in the way of telling the story. I think my writing style in characterized by a tendency to intellectualize a bit too much. In a way this impedes the flow of lyricism, which I wish I had more access to.

JD: Was there any certain part of your upbringing that has been most influential in your writing?

EGB: Certainly the storytelling. The elders were just great at this. Through their stories they taught us lessons about life, but they also entertained and opened OUR minds to the imaginary.

JD: What authors and/or literary critics' works have been influential to you?

EGB: I did my graduate work just before feminist thinking turned the canon on its head. Hence, early on, I was influenced by male writers, because that was the bulk of what I was reading. I remember being awed by Sor Juana and Santa Teresa but, alas, my introduction to them was through the perspective of male professors, and I don't think I really came to know them until much later. I remember being particularly taken by young Mexican *onda* writers. Their openness to oral language, their general irreverence, and their flair for playing with language really impressed me. Simone de Bouvoir was the first woman writer that really had an impact on my thinking. Rosario Castellanos and Luisa Valenzuela are two other writers that helped me see the world in new ways. Later writers like Ana Castillo and Denise Chávez became important influences.

JD: Is sexuality important in Chicana literature?

EGB: I think THAT given the Catholic upbringing of many Chicano writers, taking on sexuality by the horns (to use a very masculine metaphor) was crucial to finding voice. Had we not made sexuality central to our writing, we would still be donning the repressive gag of that patriarchal institution that first introduced us, in the most repressive of ways, to the body.

JD: To someone who does not know all of your work, but is familiar with a few pieces, how would you describe it? Is a common theme present in all your work?

EGB: As you know I have written very little, so it is difficult to talk about recurring themes or tendencies. I would say however, that irreverence certainly marks my work, as does irony and, as I said above, a tendency to intellectualize.

JD: Does anyone in your family write or tell stories? (I am interested in knowing how you were encouraged to write).

EGB: My mother, my father and my grandmothers were great story tellers. But none of them wrote. The truth is, I became a writer through my formal training. And this is unfortunate because this route drags along a strong internal monitor that tends to inhibit the creative writing process.

JD: Is the Chicano relationship to the dominant culture something you like to explore in your writing since you do it in *Paletitas de Guayaba*? Why is that important for Chicana literature?

EGB: Absolutely. When your whole life is lived with a clear sense of your subordination and that of others like you; when you are ever conscious of your double edged sensibility as an insider and an outsider—simultaneously—you cannot help but explore not only the meaning, but the 'work OF,' the impact and effects this unequal relationship. And if we, those of us who write from a subordinate position, are to undo the 'work' of colonialism we have to deal with it, pure and simple.

Questions about *Paletitas de Guayaba*:

JD: When you wrote *Paletitas de Guayaba*, what was your ultimate goal? What did you want to accomplish/portray with/by it?

EGB: My goal in writing *Paletitas* as simply to 'get it off my chest.' I wanted to give some order to a whole bunch of things I was experiencing and thinking about. I wrote it mainly for myself, but if it made sense to others, I would certainly be pleased. There were things I was pissed off about and I wanted the world to know, not so much that I was angry, but that things just weren't right. There was an urgency there that grew out of specific things I was going through, trying to establish myself as an academic in a very racist world.

JD: Did you consciously make the book to benefit Chican@s? Did you write the book for women?

EGB: I think I wrote this for myself. But if it spoke to other Chicanas, that was just great. I didn't pretend to speak for others.

JD: Viewing the *Paletitas de Guayaba today*, 18 years after its debut (and 3 years after its bilingual version), is there anything you would change about it to bring it up to speed?

EGB: *Paletitas* could certainly be developed more fully. It's been criticized for perhaps being too essentializing, but when it was written (1985) our ideas about identity formation, etc. were not quite as developed as they are today. It is a product of the moment in which it was written, and I think it ought to stand as testimony to that particular moment.

JD: I have included *Paletitas de Guayaba* as a part of the Chicana works I am studying—I classify these works as works by, about and for Chicanas[12387]—would you agree? That is, who was your target audience?

EGB: Certainly it was written about a Chicana and I think many Chicanas can relate to it. But I certainly would hope that it spoke to a broader audience—Mexicans for example. The language of course is a limiting factor; it presupposes a fluent Spanish reader, and that may exclude many Chican@ readers.

JD: Do you know where *Paletitas de Guayaba* has primarily been read (i.e. college classrooms, etc)? Why do you think this is so?

EGB: I think you are right. Because there are so few works written in Spanish, it is sure to be included on most reading lists in Chican@ lit. classes in Spanish Departments. Beyond that, it probably has a very limited reading public.

JD: As you know, I am including my discussion of *Paletitas de Guayaba* with two other books and three other films. I claim that *Paletitas de Guayaba* as well as the other two books are examples of Chicanisma, or the concept of "sisterhood", that is Chicana artists that give Chicanas a name, a voice and an image. Would you agree? Why or why not?

EGB: I would agree with you on this. I certainly saw this book, if ever it were published, as part and parcel of Chicana literature. I believe it shares with writers of this sub-genre a need to open up a space for Chicana voices, to deal with some of the issues that affect us a women within a specific and a broader dominant culture, and certainly to provide an image of Chicanas as intelligent, thinking human beings with a legitimate take on our experiences and on the world. Perhaps because I have written so little, and because the book may not be accessible to people who don't read Spanish, I don't always feel that I am included within the canon of Chicana writers; maybe I'm just a stepsister rather than a full-fledged member of this sisterhood. I don't know too many males who have cared for it, though there have been a few who have appreciated it.

JD: As part of your self-identification, from what point of view were you coming from when you wrote *Paletitas de Guayaba*?

EGB: I think the answer was already given under number 2. Certainly, I was exploring the character's identity as a Nuevomexicana and a Chicana. These were the two identities that I felt most connected to at the time of the writing.

JD: Does *Paletitas de Guayaba* still apply today? Why? Or why not?

EGB: I'm not sure that all of it applies today. For one thing, Mexicans look at Chican@s differently today than they did 19 years ago. There just isn't as much hostility toward Chicanos, probably because most Mexicans probably have at least one family member that's come over. Some ideas regarding identity might be a bit essentializing. In those days there was still a tendency to think of identity in more fixed rather than fluid ways. The take on Chicana sexuality may be a bit dated for today's college age reader; I don't know for sure.

JD: Why did you write this book in Spanish?

EGB: I was working in a Spanish-speaking milieu, teaching in Spanish, reading Spanish, thinking Spanish all the time. It seemed natural. Furthermore, my exposure to literature in English was limited as my studies of literature had been in a Spanish Department. What I knew of literature came from my Ph.D. studies and from teaching in a Spanish department. But there is something else. Writing in Spanish offered me a persona that was less self conscious than my narrator would have been trying to speak in English, a language I always felt deficient in, despite the fact that it is my dominant language. My language of formal education (for the Ph.D.) had been Spanish, not English, and somehow I felt more secure writing formally in Spanish. Moreover, I wasn't particularly interested in writing for a monolingual English reading audience.

JD: You said in your answer to: "Why did you write this book in Spanish?" that you weren't particularly interested in writing for a monolingual English reading audience. Can you expand on that a little more, please?

EGB: I suppose I was not interested in exposing myself to the 'gaze' of the dominant reader. I think mainstream standards have always been elusive to people who write from an 'other' social position, and I was not interested in having my work measured with the proverbial measuring stick of the power bloc. Furthermore, the things I was trying to say in that book were not necessarily meant for mainstream readers.

JD: Can you tell me a little bit more about your re-writing of La Malinche's myth?

EGB: This woman has always fascinated me. I had read some things written about her by Mexicans (i.e. Paz, Fuentes) and also by Chicanas (mainly some poems). I really wanted to continue in their trajectory of re-visioning Malinche is a more empowering way. I can't say I really wrote this section. It simply poured out on the page as if by automatic writing. This was really strange; I felt as if Malinche were really speaking through my pen.

JD: Do you believe in La Malinche? I am not sure how else to put this, but you say Malinche was really speaking through your pen (I love this comment, by the way).

EGB: Malinche was of course a historical personage—that is, she actually existed as a person. Her history fascinates me, as does her treatment by posterity. I very much believe in her. I think she was a strong woman. We will, of course, never know what motivated her actions, but it is nonetheless tempting to speculate, and that is what I have done.

JD: Do you believe that books like *Paletitas de Guayaba* that offer insight into another's culture and traditions, the U.S. society will be more accepting of each other?

EGB: Literature is a powerful tool. When I teach Chican@ lit. classes here at a predominantly white school, I am amazed at the reaction of students. They really get off on entering a world that is totally foreign to them. And I honestly believe that some bridges for understanding and tolerance are created in the process.

JD: Was there anything that was said (either by critics,

acquaintances and/or friends) about *Paletitas de Guayaba* when it first came out that really bothered you? For example, did anyone misinterpret a message in the book?

EGB: There was one review that came out in the *Albuquerque Journal* when it first came out. We (me and my comadres) were ecstatic that it was going to be reviewed. When it came out, it turned out to be a real thrashing. They had given the book to a young woman from Spain who didn't have the foggiest idea about what it meant to be a Chicana or a feminist. She did a Freudian reading of the text accusing me of being fixated on my father and of hating all cultures except my own. You cannot imagine how humiliated I was, having this kind of review come out in my home town. I tried to find out who had written the review so I could confront her personally, but no one would give me her name. Years later, I found out who it was; by then she was married to one of my colleagues! I never met her face to face; had I, I would have discussed this matter with her. To be sure, I never again spoke to the woman who ordered the review. She herself was a Chicana and I felt like she had betrayed me by giving the review to an incompetent reviewer. Diana Rebolledo wrote a wonderful, redeeming rebuttal but it was published in a hidden corner of the newspaper.

JD: What sort of response did you get after *Paletitas de Guayaba* came out in 1991?

EGB: The review (above) pretty much affected the response. People I knew just tended to pretend it had never been published and that they had never read the book! At public readings, however, the response was great.

JD: Are you surprised that someone, i.e. me, if still interested in your book 13 years later?

EGB: No, it doesn't surprise me that people would still

be interested in the book. If something is readable (and stylistically, I think it is fun) and has anything to say, people will keep reading it.

JD: Can you comment more on la "responsibilidad moral de conocer el movimiento chicano" (13)?

EGB: There was so much resistance in New Mexico to the Chicano movement. Because I personally was so affected, both intellectually and emotionally, by the movement, I believed it could have the same effect on all "Mexican-Americans or Spanish-Americans." Perhaps 'moral' responsibility was saying too much, but what I wanted to get at is that we all have a responsibility for transforming the world, particularly when it is an unjust world, and the Chicano Movement was a transformative experience which in turn empowered its followers to attempt to transform the world.

JD: In fact, you bring up several crucial Chican@ issues in the novella. Another issue is the idea of una "frontera abstracta" (29) and "*La Raza* no le gusta que le llamen *Mexican*" (29). Can you elaborate on this, please?

EGB: National borders really are abstractions, especially the U.S./Mexico border. There are places where nothing concrete separates the two countries. It is ideas about belonging and non-belonging that create borders. They are political constructs rather than natural divisions. New Mexicans have always loathed being called Mexican. Our identity as 'Spanish' was deeply entrenched, and we honestly believed that we had no connection to Mexicans. This was the result of a complex political maneuver linked to U.S. colonialism in New Mexico, but its effects were deep and regrettable.

JD: Can you comment on your references to "mexicanos" and "chicanos" in the book? What is your goal with so many references to the differences and comparisons between "mexicanos" and "chicanos"?

EGB: In the book Mexicans tend to be citizens of Mexico. Chicanos are people born in the U.S. The experiences of these two groups are quite distinct. One is a national designation used by one country to designate all of its citizens; the other an ethnic designation in a nation (U.S.) that categorized its citizens in a very unique way. Sometimes, however, Chicanos use the word mexicanos to designate their cultural identity; this draws them closer to their kin in Mexico for whom *mexicano* is a designator of national identity. Thus, the terms can be interchangeable, or they can be a mark of difference.

JD: Can you comment on the following quote, please? "Lo peor es que verdaderamente cree que las mujeres deben obedecer a sus esposos sin el menor reparo porque así lo manda la biblia" (26).

EGB: I'm no expert on the bible, but it is my understanding that women are designated therein as subordinate to their husbands. In the Catholic Church, women are taught that they cannot refuse their husband the use of their bodies should he desire to have sex. The dogma of the Catholic Church, as far as I know, is based on the bible, and from my perspective, it worked hand in hand with patriarchy in defining, controlling and containing—i.e. convents—women.

JD: Would you like to do a revision/re-write of *Paletitas*? Do you think a bilingual edition would be worthwhile? (I told Dra. Rebolledo that you should do one and have UNM press do it).

EGB: I don't see myself re-writing *Paletitas*. I would like to put out a bilingual edition, and have in fact have already translated it.

General Chican@ Questions:

JD: Were you at all involved in the Chicano or Chicana Movements?
EGB: I was indeed involved in the Chicano movement on campus at UNM. I was part of a group that designed the "Mujer Chicana" class and struggled not only with the Chicano males but also with the administration to have to accept as a legitimate class. Intellectually, politically, and emotionally, I identified completely with the Chicano Movement.

JD: What was it like being a Chicana during those years?
EGB: It was exhilarating. We truly felt empowered. For the first time in our lives we dared to take on the system and to call racism by its name. It was also exciting struggling with the brothers as we sought to carve out a space for mujeres within the movement. The struggle was not easy, but somehow we were always hopeful that we could work things out.

JD: Do you think Chicanas have progressed since the 1970s, that is, since the beginning of the Chicana Movement?
EGB: Certainly Chicanas of a certain class have progressed. There are many more professionals (professors, teachers, doctors, lawyers, businesswomen, etc.) than there were 30 or forty years ago. Chicanas, particularly those with some higher levels of education, have also progressed in their understanding of themselves as women of color and their social and cultural positioning. Things, however, have not changed that much for working class women. They still work in deplorable jobs for lousy wages, have no access to health or child care, and are still vulnerable to male exploitation and violence. Young Chicanas also seem to have lost ground in terms of issues

like self-esteem and self-image. I see far too many young girls still caught up in unhealthy ways with issues like body image. They certainly have more sexual freedom, but I don't think they have the self-knowledge, self-esteem, and gender awareness, to engage it in healthy ways. They become instead vulnerable to male whims and exploitation, and young males, of course, have not fared any better in terms of receiving enlightened sexual and gender education. There are huge gaps in the progress made by Chicanas since the Movement.

JD: Do you believe that the Chicana Movement is alive today? If so, do you think it will ever die?
EGB: I think the spirit of the Chicana movement is alive. Many of us and certainly young women today hold on the same basic tenets: the necessity to struggle against injustice and to empower our mujeres, our people and our communities through both our intellectual and our political work. So long as there is injustice, there will be political resistance, though it may not always take the form of an organized movement.

JD: What is the current plight of the Chicana in your opinion?
EGB: The biggest problem facing Chicanas today is continued sexism, pushed at all levels of culture, especially the media that makes young women experience feeling of low-self esteem. This is turn makes them drop out of school, get pregnant, thereby limiting their choices and life chances. Chicanas and Mexicanas, despite the fact that so many of them work like donkeys, cannot earn decent salaries, much less essential benefits like health care. Working class women are shamefully exploited and no one really cares.

APPENDIX H

INTERVIEW WITH FRANCES SALOMÉ ESPAÑA
El Espejo/The Mirror (1991)
Personal/Career Questions:

JD: What is your upbringing? Where/how were you raised? (With this question I am more or less interested in knowing how you got involved in filmmaking)

FSE: Fortunately or unfortunately, my own creativity has been a driving force, interest. I've always been interested in the arts, all forms. I thought about filmmaking as a young adult, even as a child, but there really didn't seem to be room for those kinds of dreams in East Los Angeles when I was growing up. Still, one keeps their dreams, makes room for them. I was a long shot, and really, I guess some might think I still am. One learns their purpose; I learned my work was in the arts, this was mine long ago.

As a child, when the family got together, an Uncle, my dad's younger brother, had an 8mm movie camera. Often he'd do screenings at our house. These are great memories for me. I really can't say that this has anything to do with my leaning toward more experimental or conceptual work—but I enjoyed them just as much, maybe more when he *re*-wound the film 'in' camera, so that we could watch each other, everybody, and everything in reverse.

I appreciate all art forms, though I've always been more of a photography, film and electronic media person. I have a collection of old cameras, gifts my parents have given me since childhood, some toy cameras, but little tools I've kept over the years, all were working cameras: an old brownie, an accordion type too, that I'd have to shoot, pull out the negative and squeegee it with a sponge of some sort to process the picture myself. A gift from my older brother, too, my first manual-only Single Lens Reflex camera, a used Miranda, I took some incredible pictures with this one. Completely absorbed in manipulating the image. I had to learn all things off this camera, because there was nothing automatic about it. But where the image in motion was concerned, it's all about access, and I had to wait until college to move into that.

JD: Was there any certain part of your upbringing that has been most influential in your filmmaking?
FSE: I really can't think of anything that I maybe haven't already included in some of your other questions. But there was love in the house.

JD: How do you identify yourself (that is, Chicana, Hispana, etc)? Why?
FSE: I identify as Chicana, Mexicana, Mexican-American. I am all of these, but I think the Chicano Movement played an important role in my self-identification as Chicana.

JD: Do you consider yourself a feminist?
FSE: Yes. Yes I do.

JD: Are you a religious person?
FSE: I believe in God. I believe in more culturally pertinent ways of expressing one's faith, that's all. God resides within me, all of us.

JD: What effects did the church and/or your family have on you growing up? How about as a woman?
FSE: I'm an artist. My parents knew this about me. I'm sure God too. Don't think the church ever had a chance.

JD: What languages did you speak growing up? Which do you speak now?
FSE: English and Spanish. My parents, perfectly bilingual, myself and my siblings, a lot less perfectly bilingual, yet I consider myself a Spanish speaker. It's a Chicano brand, obviously.

JD: Would you rather I conduct this interview in Spanish?
FSE: No. Well, you could if you want to, but I'd have to answer in English, or both.

JD: Growing up did you have a role model?
FSE: No.

JD: What about a Chicana role model?
FSE: No.

JD: How about now, do you have a role model?
FSE: No, wish I did. Although I have to say that I am inspired by many Chicana artists and writers, real dreamers, thinkers, visionaries.

JD: What filmmakers/directors and/or film critics have been influential to you? How come?
FSE: I think I've been most influenced by Paradzanov, Chris Marker, Buñuel, Cocteau, maybe Antonioni. All of these people create work that moves me emotionally, spiritually and intellectually. They are all dreamers, sensational, absurd, and painterly. Agnes Varda, Maya Deren come to mind as women filmmakers whose contributions I certainly appreciate. Closer to home, I would like to say that Lourdes Portillo's work is exceptional, and very meaningful to me.

I've met some very forward thinking people, excellent at what they do. Film/cultural critics, writers, scholars, really poets, artists in their own right. Thinkers, insightful, and helpful to my own development as an image-maker, always very supportive: Yvonne Yarbro-Bejarano, Rosa Linda Fregoso, and Carmen Huaco-Nuzum, Laura Perez, and B. Ruby Rich. These people are excellent at what they do.

JD: What inspires you to make films? How do you describe the way you make films?

FSE: The spirit moves. I don't make film/video in traditional ways. I can't afford to, to be honest. I find ways to create, and my process is abstract, but it works for me. I'm mostly a one woman operation, and usually don't need the technical expertise of others unless I'm going into an audio suite, or editing suite, where usually I'm at the mercy of the kindness of strangers... even then its after I've done all offline. Now, with the new technology, I've worked with Richard Castaniero, who was the editor for one of my new pieces. He was very good to me in the editing studio, kind, very receptive to the way I don't do things. In general I work with friends, or people I know, most of my friends are artists too, so I can ask for help with art properties, consult. I don't work with a traditional script. I make notes, write segments, and draw pictures.

JD: Did you have a difficult time getting into the film world?

FSE: Who says I ever got in? Since forever, I am my own film world. I am always going to be making my little movies. Siempre he trabajado en las afueras de todo. Maybe one day things will change, anything's possible.

JD: Does anyone in your family make films or tell stories? (I am interested in knowing how you were encouraged to make films)

FSE: I am told there was a great aunt who would ride

into Los Angeles in her old model car, who would stay for a time with her camera. She took these wonderful pictures, wonderful compositions. I have all the old photographs.

JD: Is the Chicano relationship to the dominant culture something you like to explore in your filmmaking?

FSE: Yes, but not necessarily, nor exclusively. But in the sense that bi-cultural experience is fascinating, colorful, moving, yes, and in the sense that the Chicano relationship to the dominant culture is worthy of exploration, yes.

Questions about *El Espejo/The Mirror*:

JD: Why did you want to make this film?

FSE: I wanted to do performance, it was a period of much writing, and as I mentioned in response to another question, I was doing a lot of public readings at the time. I wanted to speak to my mood, contradictions, my life and experience. I knew that it would be a good thing to just speak, to be central subject and to speak. As things transpired, it became performance for the camera. I'd never seen a Chicana speak this way on film anyway. I mean we express ourselves all the time, but except for maybe one moment or two in film history, it didn't happen for Chicanas. I didn't plan it this way initially, but I'm glad the work was transferred to film form.

JD: Why did you choose to make *El Espejo/The Mirror* a documentary?

FSE: This is an experimental piece, based on my own writing; it is an abstract, experimental piece, not a documentary. I shot it, edited it, and did my own acting for this piece. I was all alone in the middle of a room with the camera connected to my TV monitor so that I could check composition and lighting. Then I ran outside with the camera and began to shoot in the yard, and the trains too, which are further in the distance, all of this was shot at home. The yard, the chickens, the trains, it was an easy and great way to embellish the story.

JD: Is *El Espejo/The Mirror* an autobiographical portrait of you?
FSE: In a sense, yes. It began as a piece of performance art, prose writing which speaks to memory, dreamtime and experience. I thought I would use it as performance, because I was doing a lot of readings, poetry gigs back then, but I had the camera nearby, so I performed for the camera.

JD: Viewing *El Espejo/The Mirror* today, 13 years after its debut, is there anything you would change about it to bring it up to speed?
FSE: My hairdo.

JD: Does the film still apply today?
FSE: Everything but the hairdo.

JD: Why? Or why not?
FSE: Styles change.

JD: Do you know where the film has primarily been shown (i.e. College classrooms, Fine Arts Theatres)? Why do you think this is so?
FSE: Alternative art spaces, art galleries and museums, and college classrooms. I have not promoted my work in festivals. I've never had the time to do this. What happens is that occasionally I'll get a call from someone curating a segment within a film festival who asks to borrow, rent or purchase the work. I really haven't been interested in festivals as much as in making the work. I don't have time

to do both, that's all. Maybe that will change.

JD: I have included *El Espejo/The Mirror* as a part of the Chicana works I am studying—I classify these works as works by, about and for Chicanas—would you agree?
FSE: I make films that speak to my experience.

JD: Was there anything that was said (either by critics, acquaintances and/or friends) about *El Espejo/The Mirror* when it first came out that really bothered you? For example, did anyone misinterpret a message in the film?
FSE: I am open to all interpretations and analyses, receptive to all criticism. When people write about my work it's a good thing. Sometimes writers might be off mark, but I will say that this is really rare. Often because of their training in theory and criticism, relative to their own particular fields of study—they see, or say, or write things that not only hit the mark, but also, open things up, broaden the possibilities of interpretation and meaning with different ways of seeing. They can enlighten. And they are trained with the critical vocabulary that does this. I am open to all of it.

JD: Are you surprised that someone, i.e., me, is still interested in the film 13 years later?
FSE: Yes, I think it's an interesting thing. I am surprised. It's even stranger that 13 years have passed... then again on another level, I know the piece quite well and love it completely for all of its raw charm, and I think I can be an engaging actress, so no, I'm not surprised. You have good taste.

JD: Did you consciously make the film for the benefit of Chican@s? Did you choose to make this film specifically for women? That is, who was your target audience?
FSE: To date I've always wanted to use the Chicana as

central subject. No I don't have a target audience per se. My work is based on my experience, my reality. I don't feel comfortable speaking for anyone and the Chican@ experience is so diverse. I'm urban obviously, but my cultural experience includes rural, or rancho influences, tangible ones, not just memory. I think I might be a born again ranchera, well in my mind anyway, completely connected to an accordion, together in opposition to anything high-tone. And because I work very hard to transfer or translate and transform ideas, concepts, into fine art, as such, I'd like to think that the world could be my target audience.

JD: To someone who does not know all of your work, but is familiar with a few pieces, how would you describe it?
FSE: Visual poetics, experimental format, non-linear, woman centered. Conceptual, dreamtime, stunning (consider the source).

JD: Is a common theme present in all your work?
FSE: Women, agency and the transformative.

JD: When you made *El Espejo/The Mirror*, what was your ultimate goal? What did you want to accomplish/portray with it?
FSE: I am interested in working with film and video as art form. To reiterate, in *El Espejo/The Mirror*, I thought to use the camera for this performance, wanting to create something beautiful... re-working or adapting film language to Rasquachi Aesthetics and economics (see Tomas Ybarra-Frausto). I essentially worked with what I had, on limited resources and no funding to create something meaningful that I could write, direct, produce and act in, in other words, exercising complete artistic license and control on a shoe string budget.

JD: Why did you name it *El Espejo/The Mirror*? What does the mirror refer to? Also, why the bilingual title, *El Espejo/The Mirror*?

FSE: *El Espejo/The Mirror* is a concept based on ancient nahuatl philosophy, "tu eres mi otro yo," "you are my other self." The mirror is also referenced in its use by the ancient nahua sages who hold up the mirror so that we might see ourselves... reflection.

JD: Do you believe that through films like *El Espejo/The Mirror* that offer insight into another's culture and traditions, the U.S. society will be more accepting of each other?

FSE: Without taking things so seriously, I would hope first that when Chicanas see this film they are accepting of themselves. Having said this, I'd like to think that in some way this piece could provide some insight and contribute toward a greater understanding of a more diverse society.

JD: As you know, I am including my discussion of *El Espejo/The Mirror* with two others films and three others books. I claim that *El Espejo/The Mirror*, as well as the other two films are examples of Chicanisma, or the concept of "sisterhood," that is Chicana artists that give Chicanas a name, a voice and an image. Would you agree? Why or why not?

FSE: Yes. Xicanisma. To offer a rough paraphrasing of Cherrie Moraga, one of our preeminent Chicana writers: we too seek the divine within our work, challenging ourselves to produce meaning, and new ways of seeing, imagining ourselves in ways yet to be portrayed.

General Chican@ Questions:

JD: Were you at all involved in the Chicano or Chicana Movements?

FSE: I was only 16 or 17 at the time of the moratorium, but the mood and the time completely politicized and inspired me. While I was at the university I was active in many different activities, marches or political rallies. I was also involved in the woman's group, "Mujer," as well as in "MEChA." I was co-chair of Mecha with a life long friend, María Leon Vazquez, currently school board member for the city of Santa Monica.

JD: What was it like being a Chicana during those years?

FSE: I would have to say that those years were dynamic, moving and meaningful, not without faults or contradictions, but a very rich period none the less. A cultural movement was unfolding around me which provided a sense of unity, self-identification and self-determination. A significant part of this movement was an evolving Cultural Renaissance, and as an artist I was profoundly influenced.

JD: Do you think Chicanas have progressed since the 1970s, that is, since the Chicana Movement?

FSE: There is a wealth of scholarship, literature and artistic expression that is available to this generation, which was not the case in the 1970s. Subsequent generations have had access to this knowledge and are not only benefiting from this foundation but are expanding on this base of knowledge and expression in significant ways.

JD: Do you believe that the Chicana Movement is alive today? If so, do you think it will ever die?

FSE: Of course it is not the same as 30 years ago. The legacy of that time is present in a whole new generation of activists who are extremely informed and dedicated to social change, and spiritual growth, many of whom are young women artists who demonstrate this commitment in their work, in their art.

JD: What is the current plight of the Chicana in your opinion? Do you believe it has changed since *El Espejo/ The Mirror* was made?

FSE: We still have to contend, and transcend. Being a Chicana any time means we have to struggle against encumbrances and oppression of all kinds: sexism, *Machismo*, racism, social injustice and inequities, not to mention the obstacles that still remain when confronting the main stream, i.e., for the most part they still don't even know we exist. The first waves of Chicana artists and intellectuals have provided a legacy which manifests in a very empowered and dynamic younger generation of Chicana artists. The good part is that there exists a possibility for communication and creative exchange between the generations of artists whose works express an evolving Chicana aesthetic.

APPENDIX I

INTERVIEW WITH DENISE CHÁVEZ
Loving Pedro Infante (2001)
Personal/Career Questions:

JD: What is your upbringing? How did you get to the point where you wanted to write a book?

DC: Recently, I gave a workshop to Fair Acres Elementary here in Las Cruces, K-5. My cousin had given me an assignment to pull out some of my early writing and some of my art work as a child. And I have to tell you that it was really moving and startling and very empowering because I discovered I was a writer when I was 6, 7, 8. I have my very first short story which was the very beginning of "The Willow Game" in *The Last of the Menu Girls*. It was about a Willow tree that was in our yard. It was very interesting to see the photos, the artwork, to see all the diaries. My cousin who is a teacher, made some overheads of all these drawings, artwork. My parents loved to read. My father was a lawyer. My mother was a school teacher. They grew up in small, poor little towns. Their hobby was to read. My mother said that her family sat around and read newspapers. She was in a large family of eight, and they loved to read. They read newspapers; my grandfather had a lot of subscriptions to newspapers in English and Spanish. My father was a reader. I grew up with books, I loved books. One thing I showed the kids too, while I was at school was the library cards I'd made as a child. We made library cards for my dad's books in his library, and I still have them. I was always writing, teaching, doing different things. When I was in the first grade, I would come home and teach my sister, Margo, whatever

I learned. And one time my mother came home, and Margo was crying, and she said, "Denise is mad at me, it's almost Christmas, and I still can't spell things." So I was teaching her, I was her teacher. And as a result of that, she skipped a grade.

JD: Cool.
DC: YES! She owes me big time! And the thing about it is, I loved reading, I loved books, I loved storytelling, and I was able to see this and revisit this by going to the school and seeing those overheads and talking to the kids. And now as a result of that whole experience, I am working on a book called "The Writer as a Child." I would open up the diary, and I would say, "Oh my god, this is the day I got my first bra." And the kids liked hearing that, there were squeals. I had written that story for *Latina* magazine, it was called, "My First Bra". The story was about when I was 13 or 14. So I have had different versions, different flowerings, I guess you would call them, of creativity, but the same impetus. But to see that again was very profound to me. My upbringing was stories. I was surrounded by people that loved stories, so in a way, it is not surprising that I'm a story-teller.

JD: Yes, it is not surprising at all considering your mom and dad. Were they both from NM?
DC: No, my mother was from a small town in west Texas called El Polvo, The Dust. Her mother was the postmistress of El Polvo, Texas. The family loved education, they were the first Latina graduates, Hispanic graduates from Sul Ross University in Alpine, Texas. If you go on the campus, there is this wall in the middle of the campus, and they have the cattle brands of all the settlers. They were the first Latinas to graduate from that college. They were trend-setters. My mother's sister was Texas Mother of the Year, twice. Her other sister, Lucía, my Tía Chita, lived

in a very small town in west Texas at the entrance to the Big Bend area. She won many awards because she started this lending library out of her little grocery store, and people would send her books from all over the United States. She was on the Today Show and in *Parade* magazine. They were an incredible family; they were movers and shakers, just wonderful people. My mother was a very beautiful, lovely, highly intelligent, very witty person and my dad was very funny. He was like Jack Benny. He had this dry wit, highly intelligent as well. They loved current events, they loved life. They were just very interesting and motivated people.

JD: Was your dad from Texas?

DC: No, he was born Doña Ana, here in New Mexico. He grew up in Chiva Town, which is the barrio here in Las Cruces. They called it Chiva Town because there were a lot of animals over there, little goats and what have you. My dad used to talk about walking to New Mexico State through fields of rabbits; they lived practically at the end of Las Cruces. I have talked about it a lot; I always talk about it because the streets were named Mesquite, and Campo and names like this. Las Cruces has changed so dramatically. The streets didn't have fancy names—Majestic Terrace and Imperial Ridge. These were very poor Mexicanos that lived on the east side of Las Cruces, the wealthy people lived on the west and Main Street divided. They lived in the poor barrio section called Mesquite Street. Well, when you come back, Jenny, come back, but not at the Border Book Festival time. If you come back sometime, my dear, you can come and hang, and I will give you my personal tour of all of these places.

JD: I would love it.
DC: Yeah, come back with more time.

JD: You grew up in Las Cruces, right?

DC: Yes, I did. My parents divorced, my father was an alcoholic, and he was brilliant and in a way it didn't really affect his work—it did and it didn't. My parents were divorced when I was 10, and I grew up between New México and Tejas. We went back and forth, we went for holidays, and we also spent most of the summer there. So I really I grew up between states. That's literal and metaphorical too, because they were very different worlds and very interesting worlds. It was interesting because most of my mother's family spoke Spanish. My aunt refused to speak English, well I will not say refuse, but she hardly ever did. She practically refused. And then my father's family was more anglicized. They were completely, totally different worlds. But I really think that helped me become a writer and an artist because my mother's world is so charged and remote and powerful. And Las Cruces has all of those things too, but it's different. They are both very distinctive places, and I have had both of those realities which is really good.

JD: How do you identify yourself, as far as labels are concerned?

DC: I'd like to become label-less. Well, I'm Mexican-American, I'm a Mejicana in my heart and spirit. I feel comfortable with Chicana, Latina. I guess I am like Sandra Cisneros—Hispanic isn't something that rolls off my lips. I think Sandra believes and many people do, it is a word that is invented by Washington, D.C. I'm myself, I'm a woman. I'm a writer. I'm a Nuevomexicana. I try not to let labels get in my way. I am very proud to be a Mexicana to have roots in Chihuahua and to know who my people are. I think that is the most important thing is to know where you come from and where you belong. And that goes for all people. I don't want to get labeled. But I think people think that way. You're a Chicana writer, you write about the Southwest. But then when people read the work, hopefully it as universal in its truth.

JD: I agree and I think yours does, and I think that's why I was very interested in it from the onset.
DC. Ah, Jenny, thank you—

JD: Along with the Spanish...
DC: You know, today, I was talking to Liliana Valenzuela. She is a wonderful translator that translated Sandra Cisneros's book, *Caramelo*. Liliana lives in Austin. Oh we've laughed, and we've just had so much fun. She has been working through different things and asking me questions, and it's been so delightful to work with her. We're trying to get to the right words. How do you translate, "The Last of the Menu Girls" in Spanish? What does this mean and so on and so forth. I really love language. To me it is alive, and there's a lot of interplay between languages, English and Spanish. It's playful it goes back and forth. That's what I love about living in a place like New Mexico or Texas, really any place where people use language, and it's a vibrant energy.

JD: Yes, there are certain things that you cannot say in Spanish, and that you can't say in English and vise versa.
DC: Yeah, that's right—

JD: That's why I love *Loving Pedro Infante* so much.
DC: I really laughed and cried through that book. It was a wonderful book to work on. It was difficult in many ways. You know after you finish a book, it's like a dream, like a dream happened and you wake up and you go, "Oh my God what happened?" But, it was quite an exercise; I have now gotten back into my new book, *The King and Queen of Comezón*. That's what I am working on right now. I am

back writing again.
JD: Good.
DC: Yeah, I am happy.
JD: I am excited to read your next thing that comes out.

JD: Do you consider yourself a feminist?
DC: Oh, absolutely. Yes, I realized very early on in my writing life that I was writing the stories of women's lives. I think it is very important to be able to speak as a woman to women, to men, to children, to write the stories that women don't tell. I think it is like the preface I have in *Face of an Angel*. My grandmother's voice was never heard—my mother's voice, you never really heard it, but my voice is strong. I am not quoting myself very well, but it's right there at the beginning of *Face of an Angel*. I really honesty believe that I write the stories of women's lives. I have a lot of male characters, and I love men. People say, "Aren't there any good men?" I've gotten complaints; there was a guy here at New Mexico State that said, "If I didn't have to read your book, then I would have never read it." He hated it. And I said, "Well, good, I am glad you have such a disturbing response to some of the male characters in the book. Maybe we can begin to look at the relationships between men and women." This is just one story; this is not the story of all lives, all people, all men. This is *Face of an Angel* I am referring to, if this disturbs you that's okay because then we can maybe break those cyclical chains of relationship. And really, that's really the theme of *Pedro Infante*, that's Tere's story right there. I love that woman.

JD: I do, too. When you say that you tell the stories of women's lives, I mean, you do down to every detail—pulling the black hairs out of the chin.
DC: I mean down to the pores, girl.

JD: That's right.
JD: Are you a religious person?
DC: I am a spiritual person. I think that religion gets in people's way, and we become black and white and nationalistic and untrue and unfaithful to our true human nature when we become religious and fanatical. I believe in spirit, I believe that there are many paths toward enlightenment, and I have taken a few of those myself. I grew up as a Catholic; I went to Catholic school for twelve years. I always have a rosary with me. I grew up saying the rosary, as a matter of fact, the piece that I working on right now, it's called "Holding the Sacred." It is about saying the rosary, saying many hundreds and hundreds of rosaries, thousands in my lifetime because whenever we got into the car my mother would start a rosary. Every night we were on our knees on this nubby rug in front of my mother's bed hunched over saying the rosary after we did our dishes or homework, well I never did too much homework, but my mother would call us in, and we would say the rosary. And so, it was like, "God, I have got to get away from this." Gotta get away from this and what do I have in my purse? Several rosaries. When I get on an airplane I am very miedosa, I'm very frightened. What do I do? Take out my rosary.

I am putting together a short story called "Holding the Scared", and it refers to all these rosaries. In the sense of spirit, I am putting together an anthology where I want to include a lot of other writers. It will be an anthology that talks about mementos, sacred objects, sacred things that we hold close to us—whether it's that baseball mitt that you had as a boy or girl, or that rock from the Grand Canyon, that piece of bark from that tree that you loved. Whatever it was in our lives that we hold and that is scared to us. It could be an object, a nature object, a piece of cloth, whatever it is. So, I am formulating this idea for this anthology called, "Holding the Sacred". That's what I

am working on right now, the short story, and my novel.
JD: That's a great idea.
DC: It's funny. It's funny because we used to—yeah, I should include that in that, I forgot that—that's another little story that I wrote about our neighborhood. My father's cousin, Lencho Torres, had this huge, bigger than life size statue of our Lady of Guadalupe, embedded in this lava rock in his backyard. And this is what we would—
JD: (Laughing)
DC: I am not making this up, Jenny; I really am not—with Juan Diego kneeling at the Guadalupe's feet. In the summertime, this is the torture that my sister and I and all the kids in the neighborhood would be subjected to it, not only would you have to say the rosary in the car, in my mother's bed, in her bedroom, in the night around twilight, but just before twilight, we would meet to say the rosary, al fresco, at my uncle's house down the street kneeling on his concrete patio.
JD: (Laughing, still)
DC: It's a great image, huh? (Laughing)
JD: (Laughing) Uh huh, yep.
DC: Actually the house we're living in is next door to that house, and sometimes I peer over the fence, actually the cinder block wall that is there, and I see our Lady of Guadalupe. My cousin lives there with her partner, these two women, and I say, "God, Monica, what are you gonna do with the statues?" She says, "Denise, we can never remove it." So it's there, you'll have to see it someday. Actually, I have to go out there and take a picture of it.
JD: Yes, that would be great.
DC: Well, so there you have it, I cannot even remember what the question was...so, that's what spirit means to me.

JD: "Are you religious?" was the question...
DC: Yeah, spirit is aligning myself to the teachings of Thich Nhat Hanha or the Dalai Lama feeling the sense, in

my being, the sense of what spirit is or Buddhism. Or exploring my Jewish roots in México—my aunt was in the hospital, and she turned to us, Daniel [Daniel Zolinsky, Chávez's husband] and I, and she says, "We're Jewish of course". And she says, "You knew that didn't you?" and I go, "Yeah, I kind of knew that," because I felt Jewish.

JD: Right.

DC: And so that's what spirit means to me—to embrace different paths and to hold them and to be held by them at times when one needs to be held and to reach out.

JD: That's great...As far as the Catholic Church is concerned, what effects did it have on you and your family, you as a woman and you and your family?

DC: What a question.

JD: I know.

DC: What effects? You name it babe, my knees are still sore from kneeling on that rug by my mother's bed...no, and I am being facetious, the thing of it is, it has deeply impacted my life. I'm not a bitter Catholic because it's good material, not only that it's moved me, it empowered me, it's made me who I am...in good ways, in ways to be looked at very deeply, and I won't say in bad ways because I think when you grow up in a very religious environment— my mother was very devout and went to mass every day, every morning very early—you look very deeply at what religion means to people and how it effects them. It was a great education to be Catholic and to have grown up with my mother and everyone else and to have wanted to become a nun. And actually to have realized that thank god I didn't and maybe I could become a nun. At last year's Cinco de Mayo fiesta, they have a wonderful fiesta in the plaza there in Mesilla; there was a group of nuns that came from México [they come every year]. There is this one beautiful nun, I wish you could see her; they bring these rosaries and all these wonderful items. She was a widow and she became a nun in her later years. She and I got to know each other, and I enjoyed visiting her over the years and she says, "Ay, Te esperamos allí in Chihuahua" and I said, "Yes, you never know maybe I'll become a nun in my later years" who knows. And if I do, I am just going to leave, just leave Las Cruces and go into México and get lost and become a nun.

JD: Sounds like a plan...What languages did you speak growing up?

DC: Well, like I was mentioning to you. Well, it depended on who you were speaking to and where you were, what time of the day it was, and if you got up on the left side of the bed, or right. If you hurt yourself, if you said "chingao" or "oh shit" or whatever, it just depended on your mood, the time of the day, the way the stars were aligned and who you were talking to. So, I don't know it just depended.

JD: Okay, I pretty much know the answer to this question, but I am curious to know how you'll respond to it, "are you as blunt in person as you are with your writing?"

DC: Oh, even more so, god help people, yes! You know, the older I've become and the more ganas I have—I don't know, I just think I've become bolder. I think of my introduction in *The Menu Girls*, I think I have. I have just become a little bolder, maybe a little more intolerable, maybe a little wilder, I don't know. I think I have become a little more truthful. I mean, that is the ultimate goal, not to be cruel or unkind to people, but to speak truth. I know I am very grateful when I meet people that are truthful; it is such a blessing to be around people, just speak it as it is. Sometimes it is painful and hard to be around people that are truthful, but it is a relief.

JD: I agree with you completely. I've been known to be blunt and offend people, but at the same time, I get people all the time that appreciate it, so...
DC: Uh huh, I think it's a good trait.

JD: Yes, I do too. That's why I think I like you (laughing)...
DC: Yeah, that's why...

JD: You mentioned your introduction to *The Menu Girls*, is that your new version?
DC: Yes.

JD: Okay, I never got a copy of it.
DC: Well, it's out there, it came out during the Border Book Festival, as a matter fact they sold some copies there when Ana [Castillo] and I did the reading Sunday afternoon. It was a good reading, I'll tell you. I've never heard Ana Castillo stronger. But the book is out there—it's out with Vintage. The introduction, I think, touches upon what you're talking about—how do address a piece of work form 18 years ago that you go back and revisit? What's the difference then and now? Has your writing improved? Do you become better? Yes, yes, yes, yes! And it's intrinsically the same book, but I think it's stronger, you just become able to articulate, maybe, better. I think the introduction [to the new version of *The Last of the Menu Girls*] is timely as we speak, because it talks about the interplay between west Texas, Nuevo México, language, some of the themes we've been talking about right now.

JD: Oh, good.
DC: Yeah, it's a good piece. It's called "The Great Unrest"

JD: "The Great Unrest"...okay, I think in an interview

you had with Annie O. Eysturoy.

DC: Oh gosh, yes, it's been a long time, I forgot about that—

JD: She asked if you had a role model, and I am not going to say who you mentioned—
DC: Who? My mother?

JD: Yes...
DC: Oh, absolutely, I always say that she was my role model; she was a very strong woman.

JD: Okay, do you have a role model now?
DC: Yes, my mother is still my role model. Even though she's passed 21 years ago... the other night I was watching *South Pacific*, that musical movie, and I just started crying because I missed her so much. And Rosanno Brazzi, this Italian actor that she loved was in it, and I kept thinking about her and she always loved him so much, and I thought she finally got to meet Rosanno Brazzi. She was strong, intelligent, fierce, all of those things. She was just a great human being.

JD: That's awesome... what authors and literary critics' works have been influential to you?
DC: Oh gosh, the usual question.

JD: Is it really? I don't want to be a usual-question-asker.
DC: Well, no, but I think it is important to think about that, "who has influenced you?" Well, I mean, I always liked the writers that had a touch of the mystical in them, whether it was Gibran, or García Lorca or somebody like Thomas Wolf. Eugene O'Neil—tormented but powerful. A lot of my influences come from my theater background, so I've been very influenced by the Greek plays, like Euripides. I acted in all these plays. García Lorca touched

me very deeply. I think about all the plays I've been in, I mean, who needs to go even further? Chenzhou is the master of characterization and dialog, what else do you want? I was influenced by a lot of theatre people, and I mentioned mostly men because that's what we were reading and acting. But definitely, world theatre has influenced me, plays, and my own family. The women in my family have impacted me, their lives, and their stories. There are so many wonderful role models from my aunts, my mother. I didn't have to go very far off field to find strong people, you know, there are so many wonderful contemporary writers. But I think personally for me, it was my family that really made an impact on my life.

JD: That's important, that's neat. You had mentioned that you had started writing again.

DC: Well, I am always writing, but I'm talking about just having more time to just concentrate on it.

JD: Gotcha. So what inspires you to do it? Or, I mean, how do you describe the way you write?

DC: Well, I write quickly because I'm so busy now that I've gotten involved in the Cultural Center. It's like I would like to run away sometimes from the Border Book Festival or from the Cultural Center. But you know, those things are very important too, you need to have a place for people to find a home. Writing is a solitary act, but I realize that art is deeper and more profound than that, I don't want to be a selfish person; I want to interact with community and work on the healing of community. So I have immersed myself for the last 10 years or longer and in a lot of community activities. And I have to say it takes its toll, but it's a blessing, a hard blessing. So in a way, you have to balance that with your own writing. I love being alone, and that's what I love about writing, because it gives me solitude and solace.

JD: Yes...
DC: But then you need to go out, you need to share; you need to be with people. It's also very important for me. It is important that we work with men in prison or kindergarten kids, or fifth graders, or women at the battered women's shelter, whatever, whatever group we're working with. I don't know how I got into this racket, I tell you.

JD: (Laughing)
DC: (Laughing) I really do love it. Although it's exhausting, sometimes you have to balance the being in the world with the interior—the inside and out.

JD: What's a common theme present in all your work?
DC: Well, there are many. The theme of service. Are we here to serve or be served? I think that runs through *The Menu Girls* and also *Face of an Angel*. And this looking at relationships—the quality of mercy, I think my characters are merciful, they are looking for a quality of mercy, they're looking for and striving for the end to abusive relationships, they're looking for ways to clarify that illusive state of grace, they're looking for a state of grace. And that's what I do in my one woman show—I am going to mount it and travel with it this fall. I'm going to Santa Barbara—maybe you can come out there when we tape it, I'll keep you posted—

JD: Good.
DC: "Women and the State of Grace", it's called. These are different women characters of different ages, and that's what they're doing they're looking for that balance, that sense of well-being and spirit that one is always looking for. That's what life is about.

JD: Right. Do you think that you explore the Chicano relationship to the dominant culture at all? And that's an academic way of describing it...

DC: Well, yes, of course, by the very fact of being who I am. Do you feel that?

JD: Yes, I do.

DC: Okay, thank you. Thank you, Ms. Dean. Yes, you write about what you know. But I never think of a dominant culture—I don't think in that terms of dominance, because when you start thinking that way, it's like, Them and us." People keep trying to do the "them and us" thing, but I never felt—yes, sometimes you have felt the other. I remember one woman, when I was living in Dallas, said to me, "Oh, your people have such beautiful hair." I have written a piece about this, it's called "Latina Hair". How people have this kind of racist attitude about Mexicanos and their hair. And I should send it to you because it is very funny, it's a true story but kind of hard-hitting, too. Because it's ridiculous to think of hair having ethnicity, but people react to the most ridiculous things. What is Latina hair? I know people who have all different kinds of hair, so it's like Sandra Cisneros and her hair, you know, "pelitos". I try not to think in terms of dominance because I want to move away from that. But yes, I think I am a representative of culture and that's how I feel comfortable expressing myself.

JD: What about sexuality in your books?

DC: Yeah, what about it? It's there. And it makes people uncomfortable. I mean, I have people come up to me and say, "Why do you talk about breasts?" I mean, "Why? Why do you think?" Not only am I a woman, I grew up with people that had breasts that were tortured by people that taunted them—you either have too much, too little, you're this, you're that, whatever. I've been blessed and I know that and I'm very grateful for where I've been.

Questions about *Loving Pedro Infante*:

JD: As far a *Loving Pedro Infante* is concerned, did you write the book to benefit Chicanos or Chicanas?
DC: No, I don't think I did. I don't think that way; I just had a story to tell. It was about Tere's life and her seeking freedom from this dysfunctional relationship. Trying to find a way, trying to find that girl some hope, and that's what she wanted—a way out, or a way in. No, I never thought about an audience, I just thought about the character.

JD: Okay...Where has the book been primarily been read? Do you know?
DC: Ah, that I don't know. Well, let me think about that, everywhere. I hope that it has a wider audience than just the Southwest or people that love Latino or Chicano literature; I think it touches some real chords with women and relationships and trying to break free of dysfunctional relationships—find your way and become an empowered person. I have met people from all over that have read the book and that makes me happy because then I feel that it is a universal story.

JD: Yes...what sort of response have you received from people about the book? Has it been positive?
DC: Oh very much so. First of all people love Pedro Infante, let's start right there. They love him, he's such an icon to so many people from people all over the world— I've met people from Venezuela that loved him. In Europe, he was well known. People love him, so I think there's a chord that's struck there, and people really like that. So he has his fans, and in a way they kind of propelled this book. I think that it's a universal book, about an icon like

Elvis or any other person that's out there that people love deeply. So, he's helped me immensely, I thank him all the time.

JD: Were there any negative responses to the book?
DC: Well...no...I don't know, I don't think in those terms and even if I did, would I want to share that? No, I don't think negative.

JD: Okay. How come you decided to do the narrative in first person?
DC: Well, it's a first person kind of story. Remember that I have a theater background, and it's a very immediate—when you use first person—it's a very immediate sensory experience. This was Tere's story and that's how she started talking.

JD: Well, I enjoy it. At one point in the book, you're talking about people from Spain. And you write, "ethpañola," and I wanted you to elaborate on why accentuated (I have a feeling why you did) as far as the "th" for the "s" in the "Española".
DC: Oh, oh the "ethpañol" because that's how the Spanish people talk. People talk that way, I mean I'm exaggerating; I'm playing and having fun with people's language. So I mean, you know, you just have to play, writing is play, can't we play?

JD: Yes. No, I meant I got a kick out of it, I liked it.
DC: Yeah, you know, let's face it, I live in the south, people in the northern part of New Mexico, they're very Spanish, sometimes they look down on Mexicans and the people that live in this part of the world. But, you know, I don't have time for that either, that's other people's problems. But you can also always poke a little fun and deflate egos, why not?

JD: Exactly, do you think that through books like *Loving Pedro Infante* that offer insight into another's cultures and traditions that U.S. society could be accepting of other cultures?

DC: Oh, absolutely, but remember that it's a celebration of culture but it's also part of the universal fabric of life and the characters really speak to a lot of other people—it's not only Latinas or Chicanas who responded to the book, I think it has a lot to say about women and their lives. So any elucidation of a woman's innermost thoughts and spirit is welcomed. And that's what I really wanted to do.

JD: When did you write *Pedro*? It was published in 2001.

DC: Well, ah, I don't know a number of years before that. I mean, I am a slow writer. I can't remember when I began, but it took me about 4 or 5 years probably to really kick in, it just takes awhile to write a novel—it's like going to a new town and figuring out how you get to the post office, where do they have the best donuts and all that kind of stuff, so it took awhile. I don't know, maybe 4 or 5 years by the time I began it, I am not really sure anymore.

JD: You had said that you just felt the need to write about Tere's life, what was your inspiration for Tere's life?

DC: Well, just the lives of the people around me. Haven't you ever hung out at a seedy bar with a bunch of girls looking for a man?

JD: Yes (laughing)

DC: Waiting for that right person, Mr. Right or Ms. Right or whoever the right person is, to walk in the door and take you away from the boring life that you have, that you know—there's Teres everywhere, there's Irmas everywhere. I wanted to say something about the game people play looking for love, and I know it sounds kinda cliché, I really wanted to look at a character like Tere. I think she's great. She's a great person to me, I love her, I think she's a beautiful person and I applaud her strength.

General Chican@ Questions:

JD: On more general terms about your identification stuff...were you at all involved in the Chicano Movement?

DC: Well, yes and no, I mean, let's face it, I was in the Drama Department when I was going to school. Yes, I was always involved and maybe not to the extent of other people, but I was always involved in human rights' issues, working in the Drama Department. I was, you know, against the war in Vietnam, I believe that there are other ways of living. I think by living the life of an artist, you take a stand and you create peace and love and harmony and transformation, so I have always worked toward that in my work and in my pubic life, as well. I think I have become more of an activist now, but I always was working toward an understanding of what life was and trying to make it better for myself and for other people.

JD: Right...and what about the Chicana Movement that kinda came after the Chicano Movement?

DC: Well, a lot of people that I was connected with were very involved—my cousin was a Brown Beret. I mean, there was a lot going on in the 60s and 70s, I graduated from high school in '66. So, 70s, 80s, there was always a lot of swirling around, moving in and out and back and forth, and everything. I was involved, but I also submerged my involvement, perhaps, maybe in those early days more in my work, I always felt that my characters would speak the truth for me and that they would say what I needed to say, and I have always felt that. Now I've become a little more outspoken. What I need to say, I can say in my books or in my characters or in my stories. But sometimes, in times like these, you also have to stand up and write the stories that are difficult. To write and speak a true story is very difficult; people don't want to hear it. So it's a hard time for writers in a way because the media tells us to lie and artists are always the people speaking the truth. Well, not always, but we should be, we should be.

JD: Yes. Do you think that Chican@s have progressed since the 1970s, specifically Chicanas?

DC: Well, I mean, yes and no. There's still a lot of racism in the world, let's face it, but yes, things have gotten better in certain kinds of ways. Although, you know, when I look at our university, I was the first Latina writer or professor in the English Department and that was only about 8 years ago. What happened? I just feel like it's so male-dominated. There's this invisible membrane that exists in the community. The idea is that there appears to be changes and there are, there are some very good changes, but still people are struggling. People are crossing those deserts and dying out there because of the militaristic stance of the United States. People are dying, they're being killed. And who cares? We're killing our people; we're killing our youth, sending them to Iraq, let's face it, what has changed? Really, what has changed? All I can say is that some things have changed some and a lot has changed a little.

JD: Do you think that the Chicano or the Chicana movement is alive today at all?

DC: Oh, absolutely, but, you know, it is more an integral part of life. I mean, I don't think about being a Chicana, I'm just living my life here. I'm living and loving and doing what I do and being who I am. I think that there's more of a universalism and more of an acceptance of different multi-cultural backgrounds of people. I don't go around thinking, "Gee, I'm a Chicana. I'm going to think Chicana thoughts. And I'm gong to be doing this for el movimiento..."—my movimiento is life—to live, to create, to enjoy and if I'm with someone that speaks Spanish, that's what I do, or if I speak English... There is just too much time spent on politics when we could be doing so many other things.

REFERENCES

Alarcón, Norma, Ana Castillo, and Cherrie Moraga, eds. *The Sexuality of Latinas*. Berkeley: Third Woman Press, 1993.

Almaguer, Tomás. "Historical Notes on Chicano Oppression: The Dialectics of Racial and Class Domination in North America." *Aztlan: Chicano Journal of the Social Sciences and the Arts* 5.1.2 (Spring and Fall 1974): 27-47.

Anzaldúa, Gloria. *Borderlands: La Frontera: The New Mestiza*. San Francisco: Aunt Lute Books, 1999.

Barrea, Mario, Carlos Muñoz, and Charles Ornelas. "The Barrio as an Internal Colony." *People and Politics in Urban Society*. Ed. Harlan H. Hahn. Beverly Hills: Sage, 1972. 465-98.

Better, Shirley. *Institutional Racism: A Primer on Theory and Strategies for Social Change*. Chicago: Burnham Inc., 2002.

Blauner, Robert. "Internal Colonialism and Ghetto Revolt." *Social Problems* (Spring 1969): 393-408.

Brakel, Arthur. "*Paletitas de Guayaba*: Mujer chicana en la ardiente otredad." *Bilingual Review/Revista Bilingüe* 20 (May-August 1995): 128-134.

Camplis, Francisco X. "Towards the Development of a Raza Cinema (1975)." *Chicanos and Film*. Ed. Chon A. Noriega. New York: Garland, 1992. 284-302.

Castillo, Ana. *Massacre of Dreamers*. Plume, 1995.

- - -. "Massacre of Dreams: Essays on Xicanisma." *Chicana Feminist Thought: The Basic Historical Writings*. Ed. Alma M. García. New York: Routledge, 1997. 310-312.

Chabram-Dernersesian, Angie. "I Throw Punches for My Race, but I Don't Want to Be a Man: Writing Us—Chicanos (Girl, Us)/Chicanas—into the Movement Script." *Cultural Studies* Eds. Lawrence Grossberg, Cary Nelson and Paula Lieichlee. New York: Routledge, 1992. 81-95.

Chávez, Denise. *Loving Pedro Infante*. New York: Washington Square Press, 2001.

- - -. Personal Interview. 10 May 2004.

Chávez, John. *The Lost Land: The Chicano Image of the Southwest*. Albuquerque: University of New Mexico Press, 1984.

Chicana. Dir. Sylvia Morales. Narr. Carmen Zapata. Women Make Movies, 1979.

"Chicana Newspaper: 'Hijas de Cuatemoc'". *Hijas de Cuatemoc* (April 1971): 2.

Cota-Cárdenas, Margarita. *Puppet*. Albuquerque: The University of New Mexico, 2000.

- - -. Personal Interview. 16 May 2004.

- - -. "Re: more puppet." E-mail to Jennifer Dean. 22 April 2003

- - -. "Re: Puppet and my final paper at UNM." E-mail to Jennifer Dean. 25 Nov 2002.

Cotera, Marta. "Among the Feminists: Racist Classist Issues—1976." *Chicana Feminist Thought: The Basic Historical Writings*. Ed. Alma M. García. New York: Routledge, 1997. 213-220.

- - -. "Feminism: The Chicano and Anglo Versions—a Historical Analysis." *Chicana Feminist Thought: The Basic Historical Writings*. Ed. Alma M. García. New York: Routledge, 1997. 223-231.

Del Olmo, Frank. "Hispanic, Latino or Chicano?: A Historical Review." *Latinos in the United States: A Resource Guide for Journalists*. Detroit: Knight Ridder Newspapers: 2001. 9-12.

Domínguez, Christine. "The Daughters of Aztlán: A Socio-Historical Survey of Chicanas in the United States". *Berkeley McNair Journal* 2 (Summer 1994): 120-129.

Durán, Livie I., and Bernard H. Russell. "Introduction: La Raza and Chicano History." *Introduction to Chicano Studies*. Eds. Livie L. Durán and H. Russell Bernard. New York: Macmillan, 1982. 1-12.

España, Frances Salomé. "On Filmmaking: A Personal Odyssey." *Chicana (W)rites: on Word and Film*. Ed. María Herrera-Sobek and Helena María Viramontes. Berkeley, CA: Third Woman Press, 1995. 275-278.

- - -. Personal Interview. 16 May 2004.

El Espejo/The Mirror. Dir. Frances Salomé España. Frances Salomé España, 1991.

"El Movimiento and the Chicana: What Else Could Breakdown a Revolution But Women Who Do Not Understand True Equality." *La Raza* 1.6 (1971): 40-42.

Eysturoy, Annie O. "Interview with Denise Chávez." *This Is About Vision: Interviews with Southwestern Writers*. Eds. Balassi, William and John F. Crawford and Annie O. Eysturoy. Albuquerque: The University of New Mexico Press, 1990. 157-169.

Falicov, Tamara L. "Lourdes Portillo." Ian Aitken, Ed. *Encyclopedia of Documentary Film*. London and New York: Routledge, forthcoming, September 2005.

Fitzsimons, Connie. "LA Freewaves: Celebrating the Existence of Independent Video." *Artweek* (December 7, 1989): 20.

Fregoso, Rosa Linda. "Chicana Film Practices: Confronting the 'Many-headed Demon of Oppression'." *Chicanos and Film*. Ed. Chon A. Noriega. New York: Garland, 1992. 189-204.

- - -. "La Quinceañera of Chicana Counter-Aesthetics." *Centro de estudios puertorriqueños bullentin* 3.1 (Winter 1991): 87-91.

- - -, ed. *Lourdes Portillo: The Devil Never Sleeps and Other Films*. Austin: University of Texas, 2001.

- - -. *The Bronze Screen*. Minneapolis: University of Minnesota Press, 1993.

Galindo, Letticia D. and María Dolores Gonzáles, eds. *Speaking Chicana: Voice, Power and Identity.* Tucson: The University of Arizona Press, 1999.

García, Alma M., ed. *Chicana Feminist Thought: The Basic Historical Writings.* New York: Routledge, 1997.

- - -. "The Development of Chicana Feminist Discourse 1970-1980." *Gender and Society* 3.2 (June 1989): 217-238.

Gladden, Dorinda Moreno. "Church and Family." *Hijas de Cuahtemoc* (April 1971): 2.

Gonzáles-Berry, Erlinda. *Paletitas de Guayaba.* Albuquerque: El Norte Publications, 1991.

- - -. "Re: *Paletitas de Guayaba.*" E-mail to Jennifer Dean. 21 Nov 2002.

- - -. Personal Interview. 13 April 2004.

- - -. "Searching for a Voice: Ambiguities and Possibilities." *Speaking Chicana: Voice, Power and Identity.* Eds. D. Letticia Galindo and María Dolores Gonzáles. Tuscon: The University of Arizona Press, 1999. 123-133.

Gutiérrez-Jones, Carl. *Rethinking the Borderlands: Between Chicano Culture and Legal Discourse.* Berkeley: University of California Press, 1995.

Gutiérrez, Ramón A. "Community, Patriarchy, and Individualism: The Politics of Chicano History and the Dream of Equality". Vicki L. Ruiz and Ellen Carol DuBois, eds. *Unequal Sisters: A Multiculural Reader in U.S. Women's History.* New York: Routledge, 2000: 587-606.

Huaco-Nuzum, Carmen. "Testimony and Bearing Witness." *Quarterly Review of Film & Video* 18.1 (2001): 83-90.

Kotz, Liz. "Unofficial Stories: Documentaries by Latinas and Latin American Women." *Centro de estudios puertorriqueños bullentin* 2.8 (1990): 58-69.

La Ofrenda: The Days of the Dead. Dirs. Lourdes Portillo and Susana Muñoz. Narr. Carmen Zapata. Direct Cinema Limited, 1988.

Mar-Molinero, Clare. *The Politics of Language in the*

Spanish-Speaking World: From Colonisation to Globalisation. London: Routledge, 2000.

Martínez, Elizabeth, and Ed McCaughan. "Chicanas and Mexicanas within a Transitional Working Class." *Between Borders: Essays on Mexicana/Chicana History*. Ed. Adelaida Del Castillo. Encino: Floricanto Press, 1990. 51.

Martínez, Jacqueline M. "Speaking as a Chicana: Tracing Cultural Heritage through Silence and Betrayal." *Speaking Chicana: Voice, Power, and Identity*. Eds. D. Letticia Galindo and María Dolores Gonzáles. Tucson: The University of Arizona Press, 1999. 59-84.

Mathiessen, Peter. *Sal Si Puedes (Escape If You Can)*. Berkeley: The University of California Press, 2000.

Melville, Margarita B. *Twice a Minority: Mexican-American Women*. St. Louis: Mosby Press, 1980.

Mirandé, Alfredo, and Evangelina Enríquez. *La Chicana: The Mexican-American Woman*. Chicago: The University of Chicago Press, 1979.

Mirandé, Alfredo. *The Chicano Experience: An Alternative Perspective*. Notre Dame, IN: University of Notre Dame Press, 1985.

Morales, Sylvia. "Filming a Chicana documentary (1979)." *Chicanos and Film*. Ed. Chon A. Noriega. New York: Garland, 1992. 341-344.

- - -. Personal Interview. 13 May 2004.

Moya, Paula M. L. *Learning from Experiences: Minority Identities, Multicultural Struggles*. Berkeley: University of California Press, 2002.

Muñoz, Carlos. *Youth, Identity, Power: The Chicano Movement*. New York: Verso, 1989.

Muñoz, Susana Blaustein. Personal Interview. 1 May 2004.

Newman, Kathleen. "Steadfast Love and Subversive Acts." *Visible Nations: Latin American Cinema and Video*. Ed. Chon A. Noriega. Minneapolis, MN: University of Minnesota Press, 1992. 285-301.

Nieto, Consuelo. "The Chicana and the Women's Rights Movement". *La luz* 3.6 (September 1974): 10-11.

Nieto, Nancy. "Macho Attitudes." *Hijas de Cuahetmoc* (May 1971): 4.

Nieto-Gomez, Anna. "La Feminista." *Encuentro femenil* 1.2 (1974) 34-47.

Noriega, Chon A. "Between a Weapon and a Formula: Chicano Cinema and Its Contexts." *Chicanos and Film: Representation and Resistance*. Ed. Chon A. Noriega Minneapolis: The University of Minneapolis Press, 1992. 141-167.

Noriega, Chon. *Chicanos and Film: Resistance and Representation*. Minneapolis: University of Minnesota Press, 1992.

Núñez-Noriega, Guillermo. *Modernidad y sexualidad en dos proyectos culturales mexicoestadounidenses": el acomodacionismo y el feminismo*. Thesis (Ph. D.). Tempe: Arizona State University, 1994.

Orozco, Aurora E. "Mexican Blood Runs Through My Veins." *Speaking Chicana: Voice, Power and Identity*. Eds. D. Letticia Galindo and María Dolores Gonzáles. Tuscon: The University of Arizona Press, 1999. 106-122.

Phillips, Melody. "The Chicana: Her Attitudes Towards the Woman's Liberation Movement." *Comadre* 2 (Spring 1978): 42-50.

Portillo, Lourdes. "On Chicanas and Filmmaking: a Commentary." *Chicana (W)rites: on Word and Film*. Eds. María Herrera-Sobek and Helena María Viramontes. Berkeley, CA: Third Woman Press, 1995. 279-282.

- - -. Personal Interview. 10 May 2004.

Rashkin, Elissa J. "Historic Image/Self-Image: Reviewing *Chicana*." *Genders 25: Sex Positives? The Cultural Politics of Dissident Sexualities*. Eds. Thomas Foster, Carol Siegel, Ellen E. Berry. New York: New York University Press, 1997. 97-119.

Rebolledo, Tey Diana, and Eliana Rivero, eds. *Infinite*

Divisions: An Anthology of Chicana Literature. Tucson: The University of Arizona Press, 1993.

Rebolledo, Tey Diana. Introduction. *Puppet*. By Margarita Cota-Cárdenas. Albuquerque: The University of New Mexico, 2000. xiii-xxii.

- - -. Introduction. "Creating Sanctuaries of the Heart: An Introduction." *Sanctuaries of the Heart/Sanctuarios del Corazon: A Novella in English and Spanish*. By Margarita Cota-Cárdenas. Tucson: The University of Arizona Press, 2005.

- - -. *Women Singing in the Snow: a Cultural Analysis of Chicana Literature*. Tucson: The University of Arizona Press, 1995.

Rinderle, Susan. "Quienes son/quienes somos: A Critical Analysis of the Changing Names of People of Mexican Descent across History." Unpublished essay.

Robles, Erika. "Is the term Hispanic a race?" Available on-line: <http://www.geocities.com/oakspublishing/race.html> Accessed: 3/24/04.

Salazar, Rubén. "Who Is a Chicano? And What Is It the Chicanos Want?" *Los Angeles Times* 6 February 1970: II-7.

Saldívar-Hull, Sonia. *Feminism on the Border: Chicana Gender Politics and Literature*. Berekley: The University of California Press, 2000.

Sánchez, Rita. "Chicana Writer Breaking Out of the Silence." *Chicana Feminist Thought: The Basic Historical Writings*. Ed. Alma M. García. New York: Routledge, 1997. 66-68.

Sánchez, Rosaura. "Deconstructions and Renarrativizations: Trends in Chicana Literature." *La revista bilingue* 21.1 (1996): 52-58.

Segura, Denise A. and Beatriz M. Pesquera. "Beyond Indifference and Antipathy: The Chicana Movement and Chicana Feminist Discourse." *Aztlán* 19.2 (Fall 1988-1990): 69-92.

Shuru, Xochitl Estrada. *The Poetics of Hysteria in*

Chicana Writing: Sandra Cisneros, Margarita Cota-Cárdenas, Pat Mora, and Bernice Zamora. Thesis (Ph. D.). Albuquerque: The University of New Mexico, 2000.

Stern, Gary M. "Why the Dearth of Latino Directors?" *Cineaste* 19.2-3 (1992): 45-47.

Tafolla, Carmen. *To Split a Human: mitos, machos y la mujer chicana*. San Antonio, TX: MACC, 1985.

Tatum, Beverly Daniel. *Why Are All the Black Kids Sitting Together in the Cafeteria?* Basic Books, 2003.

Tatum, Charles M. *Chicano Popular Culture: Que hable el pueblo*. Tucson: The University of Arizona Press, 2001.

---. *La literatura chicana*. Traducción al español: Víctor Manuel Velarde. México, D.F.: Consejo Nacional de Fomento Educativo, 1986.

Ugarte, Sandra. "Societal Perspective of Oppresion." *Hijas de Cuahtemoc* (April 1971): 2.

Velasco, Juan. "The Cultural Legacy of Self-Consciousness: An Interview with Lourdes Portillo." *Journal of Latinos and Education* 1.4 (2002): 245-253.

Vidal, Mirta. *Chicanas Speak Out Women: New Voice of La Raza*. New York: Pathfinder Press, 1971.

Villarreal, Javier. "El mestizaje lingüístico manifestaciones socioculturales en *Puppet* de Margarita Cota-Cárdenas." *Confluencia: Revista hispánica de cultura y literatura* 16.2 (Spring 2001): 24-31.

Yarbro-Bejarano, Yvonne. "Chicana Literature From a Chicana Feminist Perspective." *Chicana Creativity and Criticisim: New Frontiers in American Literature*. Eds. María Herrera-Sobek and Helena María Viramontes. Albuquerque: University of New Mexico Press, 1996.

Notes

[12337]
For, by and about Chicanas is an idea Rosa Linda Fregoso discusses in her book, *The Bronze Screen.* This concept includes all the women and works discussed herein with the exception of Susana Blaustein Muñoz, who is from Argentina—although she identifies as Latino-Jewish, she believes her work with Lourdes Portillo, *La Ofrenda*, is by Chicanas (Personal Interview 5/1/04).

[12338]
When the designation Chican@ is used, it refers to the group of people in the neutral sense, not their specific genders and/or sexes.

[12339]
Race is a social construction imposed on groups of people by American society. Classically, American society groups an individual in a certain race according to the color of her/his skin color. Likewise, an individual can be grouped into a racial category because of the combination of, but certainly not limited to: his/her religion, language, national origin and/or cultural differences. However, these categories are really categories that define or set-off one's ethnicity (Better 19).

[12340]
The origins of the word are controversial, no one really knows why the term caught on and is so widely used today (Del Olmo 10).

[12341]
This point is addressed later on in Chapter 6: Racism in

American Society and the Chicana.

[12342] In the 1960s, during the Chicano Movement "young people adopted the once-disreputable term Chicano as a symbol of pride and self-assertion" (Del Olmo 11). Chicanos then and now see themselves as descendents from Aztlán, the mythical homeland of Chican@s, the part of the U.S. that was once part of Mexico, and therefore non-Anglo.

[12343] Muñoz "was one of the organizers of the Los Angeles student strike and one of the thirteen men indicted for conspiracy, and [...]played a leadership role in the development of the student and Chicano Power movements" (Muñoz xiii).

[12344] This is discussed in detail in the next chapter.

[12345] To read more about the internal colonial theory (in addition to the sources used in this work) see: Almaguer, Tomás. "Toward the Study of Chicano Colonialism." *Aztlan* 2.1 (Spring 1971): 7-21.

[12346] Though it is beyond the scope of this work to discuss the neocolonialism and the internal colony in detail, it is discussed briefly in hopes that it will be researched further by those interested. Almaguer, Tomás. "Historical Notes on Chicano Oppression: The Dialectics of Racial and Class Domination in North America." *Aztlan: Chicano Journal of the Social Sciences and the Arts* 5.1.2 (Spring and Fall 1974): 27-47 and "Toward the Study of Chicano Colonialism." *Aztlan: Chicano Journal of the Social Sciences and the Arts* 2.1 (Spring 1971): 7-21. As well as, Blauner, Robert.

"Internal Colonialism and Ghetto Revolt." *Social Problems* (Spring 1969): 393-408

12347
Many Chicanas have reported being punished for speaking Spanish. Aurora Orozco in her article, "Mexican Blood Runs through My Veins", claims, "[w]e were prohibited from speaking Spanish in class and on the playground, but everyone spoke Spanish behind the teacher's back. I was one of those students who spoke Spanish in class, so my teacher, Mrs. White, would make me stay after class. With a red rubber band, she would hit my poor hands until they nearly bled" (110).

12348
As discussed in the previous chapter.

12349
The concept of Chicanisma in this work is not the same as the Xicanisma (politically and socially active feminism) Ana Castillo discusses in her *Massacre of the Dreamers*.

12350
Mexican-Americans became the conquered people of the war between Mexico and the United States.

12351
As members of the working-class, many Chican@s could not afford to risk their jobs to strike and form a labor union. After all, many Chican@s live day-to-day on their pay checks; therefore, the risk involved in losing a job was often too great. Often the battle for economical survival was more important than the fight for human and civil rights. Yet, the success of the grape boycott finally broke the mold—Chican@s were inspired by its success.

12352
Part of the idea of Chicanismo was the concept of Aztlán, which is the mythical homeland for the Chican@

people. Aztlán represents the struggle of Chican@s in the pasts, who continue to struggle in the present to guarantee their future.

¹²³⁵³ *La Virgen de Guadalupe* is considered the indigenous version of the Virgin Mary. "As the paradigmatic spirit of female sexual and personal abnegation, *La Virgen* is the revered mother and patron saint of Mexico" (Moya 64). When there are references to La Llorona or to La Malinche the images are usually negative (Rebolledo and Rivero 192). La Malinche is discussed further in Chapter 4. Similar to La Malinche, La Llorona symbolized the unnatural maternity and the inappropriate sexual desire of women. In order to find more information in regards to archetypal figures, *La Virgen de Guadalupe*, La Llorona and La Malinche, see the fifth chapter, "Myths and Archetypes" (189-195) en *Infinite Divisions*.

¹²³⁵⁴ Of course, Chávez, Huerta and the UFW had been accused of being communists—a label one wanted to avoid in the 1960s.

¹²³⁵⁵ However, later on, through literature and film, Chicanas would fight to dispel these myths and archetypes that had subordinated them.

¹²³⁵⁶ "The word *macho* means to be male or masculine. *Machismo*, therefore is that which is related to the male or to masculinity. *Machismo*, as associated with Mexican culture for the social scientist, is the demonstration of physical and sexual powers and is basic to self-respect [. . .] one could not define *Machismo* as idiosyncratically Mexican, or Latino for that matter." (Castillo *Massacre of the Dreamers*

66). "...*Machismo* is an exaggerated demonstration of male virility that is inherent in most cultures, but is exemplified most in the United States by their own Anglo leaders" (*Massacre of the Dreamers* 14).

Nieto-Gómez's voice continues to be expressed in Chicana feminist theory today.

It comes as no surprise that *Chicana* mentions that "We [Chicanas] fight for better working conditions, education, welfare rights..." (Video) which were central issues to the Chicana Feminist Movement.

Unlike Chicano or Anglo writers, Chicana writers use a first person narrator in many cases, making for a more personable and real life character (Mirandé and Enríquez 179).

Since *Puppet* was originally written in Spanish, I find it necessary to include the original version of the passages in Spanish and its translation in English. This small excerpt of the chapter does not do it justice and to understand it fully, it is best to read the chapter in entirety.

The telephone in the novel functions as reality maker—it breaks the circle of paranoia and brings Petra into reality.

Gaspar Alba makes this comparison in her poem "Making Tortillas" (Rebolledo 143, 1995). Additionally, Cota-Cárdenas adds that "When Petra answers the phone, she's been interrupted from her "romanticaca" mode, which she goes into as one way to escape the pressure of

what's going on in her "real" world (Puppet, the fear, the memories, the self-questioning etc.).
So she says she was "just making tortillas" as a way of saying "just fooling around, putzing" [...] Petra was kind of playing a mental game with herself, to avoid thinking of the really heavy stuff going on with her and around her at that time" (25 Nov 2002).

12363
"...it is significant that the presence in both these texts of Malinche and her "discursos" emphasizes the authors' final seizing of power. For both Cota-Cárdenas and Gonzáles-Berry, Malinche appears as "la lengua" (the tongue) and represents an appropriation of the language, the power to write, and female subjectivity as well as female sexuality" (Rebolledo 181, 1995).

12364
"As Norma Alarcón has noted, the terms *traitor* and *translator* collapse in Chicano cultural iconography inasmuch as La Malinche (Cortez's native interpreter) has traditionally been made the paradigmatic figure of feminine betrayal. While there is a great deal of supposition about La Malinche's history [...] there is little doubt that she has acted as a principal reference point for the masculinist cultural production of Chicano shame" (Gutiérrez-Jones 109-110).

12365
It is important to read the chapter in entirety in order to have a firm grasp on what Cota-Cárdenas does with the myth of La Malinche.

12366
Cota-Cárdenas also makes reference to Malinche's "COMADRE LLORONA" (103) further expressing her demystification of traditional archetypes.

"...'huevos-ovarios' [is] saying that women have to be as strong as any man, if not doubly strong, often in going on with their lives and struggles" (Personal e-mail 11/25/02).

In an e-mail, Cota-Cárdenas mentioned why the book was translated into English: "For a wider reading audience, we decided to get the book translated into English, and in this way, a non-Spanish speaking reader say in Sweden, or Wales (England), and even Russia and Germany can read the book. So, the small press, even self-publishing broke open the reader opportunities, and we went further by doing it in English. Now they know there are other writers besides Cisneros, Castillo, Chávez, Martínez (who are immediately highly 'marketable' with established or big presses just simply because of the language question, and of course talent). [...] We became 'pragmatic', simply put. But if I write in one language first, the translations are only 'renderings' and most usually don't do justice to what the writer does in the original language of choice—or inspiration" (Cota-Cárdenas 22 April 2003).

The film done in 1985 won 20 awards. It tells the story of the mothers who, during Argentina's Dirty War (a dictatorship from 1976-1983), made heroic efforts for the desaparicidos ("disappeared" children) (Falicov 1).

The female narrator in *La Ofrenda* is Carmen Zapata, who also narrated *Chicana*.

This is evident in the film when an older man is interviewed and asked if he is scared of the dead (because he happens to be standing where their souls rest), he replies with a laugh, "No... ¿por qué?" In fact the concept of death and fear is so far-fetched in Mexican society that the children around him laugh as well.

12372
Also addressed in this theme is the idea of Anglo oppression. Their oppression stems from Anglo ignorance, nativism and ethnocentrism—racist practices that have been prevalent for more than a century in this country.

12373
The cross-dresser in the film mentions, "*la ofrenda es una palabra de amor y el amor no tiene precio. La ofrenda sigue*" (Video).

12374
Both Mexicans and Chican@s have an indigenous background, and they are often linked because of this.

12375
"Marina [...] goes beyond merely telling her story: she seizes the language by appropriating male public language and imposing on that language the alterity, or otherness, of speaking the female body, of speaking female sexuality. In addition, she subverts the mythology of male body parts and by laughing at the mythology. By so doing, Gonzáles-Berry not only has seized the language but has undermined and overturned it, thus controlling the power of this language. She continues to demystify masculine power
[...] by articulating and speaking out female desires and needs" (Rebolledo 177, 1995).

12376
Like in *Puppet*, the encounter with La Malinche occupies an entire chapter (Gonzáles-Berry 71-77, 1991).

Also, an English version of the chapter appears in *Infinite Divisions*, like that of *Puppet*.

Of course, the name "Marina" holds connotations of La Malinche in itself.

"Chicana scholars have been especially insistent on rereading what Norma Alarcón (1983) calls the "male mythology of *La Malinche*." It is through the demystifying of La Malinche that scholars [...] have forced a reconsideration of the "loyalist versus betrayer" binarism, especially as it is tied to Chicanas' sexuality" (Martínez 79).

"...religion also plays a very important role in controlling female sexuality and reining in female desire. Historically it did this by offering a place where women could be locked up and protected—the conventos—whether or not they were nuns. And it does so by confession. I think the fear of authority that is inculcated in our culture, and the shame of confessing TO A MAN one's sexual desire/actions is one way of keeping women in a state of virginity. Also, for my generation, we grew up in a culture in which the code was very clearly defined and all members of the community played by these rules: THERE WERE GOOD GIRLS AND THERE WERE BAD GIRLS: AKA: PUTAS. Parents knew this, girls knew this, and boys knew this. If a boy took out a "good girl" he knew just how far he could go, and he didn't expect or pressure girls to go beyond that point—lots of necking (see this in the *Paletitas*). With putas, there were no limits." (Gonzáles-Berry 2002)

In the April 1971 edition of *Hijas de Cuahtemoc*, Sandra Ugarte confesses, "The church has worked to hinder and oppress the woman in many ways [...] The Church has oppressed [her] by defining and limiting her role. Such phrases as Hija de La Chingada, Hija de Malinche, and Hija de María are example of this" (2).

[^12381]
"My point in the book is that the label puta is a way to control women; to keep them from becoming independent and to prevent them from deciding what they want to do with their bodies. What I am trying to say here is that my books talks back to two "master narratives": patriarchy, and religion.

Michel Foucault talks about the role of confession as an instrument of power designed to control/police the human body. Exerting power and policing societies always is linked to the power structures ability to inflict punishment to the human body. Hence social control depends on the control of our physicality, including sexuality." (Gonzáles-Berry 2002).

[^12382]
In addition to referring to multiple birth control methods that she has tried, including the diaphragm, La Tere talks about "*Machismo*" on page 52. Both "*Machismo*" and birth control were strong issues of the Chicana Feminist Movement, therefore it is not surprising that they are found within Chávez's text.

[^12383]
Susana Blaustein Muñoz excluded here.

[^12384]
This is Jennifer Dean's transcription from the video. The spaces represent pauses in the testimonio during the video.

[^12385]
By, about and for Chicanas is a concept that Rosa Linda

Fregoso discusses in her book, *The Bronze Screen*.

[12386]
By, about and for Chicanas is a concept that Rosa Linda Fregoso discusses in her book, *The Bronze Screen*.

[12387]
By, about and for Chicanas is a concept that Rosa Linda Fregoso discusses in her book, *The Bronze Screen*.

Index

Blaustein Muñoz, Susana, pgs. 5, 79, 155, 232, 241.
Border crossing, pgs. 21, 26, 29, 42, 80, 83, 222.
Catholicism and the Catholic Church, pgs. 31, 32, 33, 34, 35, 44, 92, 93, 125, 144, 167, 177, 178, 179, 181, 189, 209, 211.
César Chávez, pgs. 37, 49, 152.
Chávez, Denise, pgs. 5, 7, 9, 11, 12, 68. 106, 114, 115, 181, 203, 226.
Chicana (1979), pgs. 11, 12.
Chicana (Defined), pgs. 20, 21, 23, 24, 26, 27.
Chicana Feminist Movement, pgs. 36, 42, 43, 46, 49, 50, 51, 65, 66, 69, 236.
Chicana Movement, pgs. 191, 222.
Chicana Sexuality, pgs. 185; see also Sexuality
Chicanisma (Defined), pgs. 9, 10, 11, 12, 36, 51, 52, 78, 99, 113, 114, 136, , 137, 159, 184, 200, 234.
Chicanismo, pgs. 36, 38, 39, 43, 45, 234.
Chicano Movement, pgs. 36, 38, 39, 43, 45, 234.
Cisneros, Sandra, pgs. 68, 72, 206, 217, 230, 238.
Civil Rights Movement, pgs. 23, 37, 39, 46, 55, 128, 170, 234.
Code-switching/bilingualism, pgs. 67, 113, 116.
Cota-Cárdenas, Margarita, pgs. 7, 11, 12, 67, 68, 69, 70, 72, 73, 74, 75, 76, 78, 89, 94, 95, 96, 97, 106, 110, 114, 115, 143, 153, 225, 230, 231, 236, 237, 238.
Crossing borders. See Border crossing.
Days of the Dead, The, pgs. 11, 79, 81, 82, 85, 86, 87, 88, 11, 155, 157, 159, 162, 168, 169, 227.
Doña Marina. See La Malinche, pgs.
El Espejo/The Mirror (1991), pgs. 11, 99, 101, 104, 106, 114, 122, 192, 196, 197, 198, 199, 200, 226.

España,Frances Salomé, pgs. 7, 11, 12, 99, 114, 115, 118, 192, 226.
Feministas, pgs. 42, 43, 44.
Gonzáles-Berry, Erlinda, pgs. 7, 11, 12, 66, 68, 77, 79, 89, 90, 91, 92, 94, 95, 96, 97, 98, 106, 110, 113, 114, 115, 118, 177, 227, 237, 239, 240, 241.
Hispanic (Defined), pgs. 14, 15, 16, 17, 24, 63, 79, 124, 149, 204, 206, 225, 230.
Homosexuality, pgs. 44, 81, 86, 87, 88, 115, 159, 171.
Huerta, Dolores pgs. 37, 49, 63.
I Am Joaquín (1969), pgs. 56, 57, 58, 133, 137.
Internal Colonial Theory, pgs. 27, 28, 29, 101, 102, 104, 115, 124, 133, 134.
King, Martin Luther, pgs. 37.
La Causa, pgs. 37, 38, 39.
La Llorona, pgs. 40, 97, 110, 235.
La Malinche, pgs. 40, 41, 57, 58, 59, 60, 61, 62, 70, 72, 73, 74, 75, 78, 94, 95, 96, 97, 110, 137, 150, 186, 235, 237, 239, 240.
La Ofrenda: The Days Of The Dead (1998), pgs. 159, 160, 162, 166, 168, 169, 170, 173, 174, 227, 232, 238, 239.
La Raza, pgs. 34, 39, 40, 113, 188, 226, 231.
La Virgen de Guadalupe, pgs. 31. 40. 58, 111, 235,
Latina (Definition), pgs. 12, 20, 53, 54, 115, 116, 131, 146, 147, 148, 153, 204, 206, 217, 221, 222, 223, 224.
Loving Pedro Infante (2001), pgs. 9, 11, 12, 106, 107, 108, 111, 113, 114, 116, 117, 203, 207, 218, 220, 225.
"Loyalists," pgs. 42, 44.
Machismo, pgs. 44, 45, 46, 119, 146, 202, 235, 236, 241.
Malintzín Tenepal, *See* La Malinche..
Mexican American (Definition), pgs. 14, 16, 17, 18, 19, 20, 23, 24, 29, 37, 38, 51, 60, 72, 128, 188, 193, 206, 228, 234.
Mora, Pat, pgs. 68, 72, 144, 231.

Morales, Sylvia, pgs. 228.
Muñoz, Susana, pgs. 7, 11, 12, 53, 57, 63, 114, 115, 117, 124, 225.
Neocolonialism, pgs. 28, 29, 233.
Nieto-Gómez, Anna, pgs. 42, 43, 47, 48, 49, 50, 54, 58, 130, 132, 133, 236.
Paletitas de Guayaba (1991), pgs. 11, 67, 89, 90, 92, 94, 96, 97, 106, 114, 177, 182, 183, 184, 186, 187, 224, 227.
Portillo, Lourdes, pgs. 7, 11, 12, 53, 79, 80, 83, 87, 114, 115, 160, 162, 194, 226, 227, 231, 232.
Puppet: A Novella (1985), pgs. 65, 68, 69, 70, 72, 73, 75, 76, 77, 78, 79, 90, 106,, 11, 114, 143, 145, 146, 147, ,148, 149. , 150, 151, 152, 154, 225, 230, 231, 237, 239, 240,
Salomé España, Frances, pgs.
Sexuality, pgs. 27, 31, 66, 67, 70, 75, 76, 87, 90, 92, 93, 96, 97, 107, 108, 140, 146, 157, 171, 181, 185, 217, 237, 239, 240, 241.
Sor Juana Inés de La Cruz, pgs. 63, 150, 180.
Treaty of Guadalupe Hidalgo, pgs. 26, 37.
Triple Oppression, pgs. 10, 21, 35, 36, 102, 115.
UFWU (United Farm Workers' Union), pgs. 37, 38, 40, 49, 235.
Viramontes, Helena María, pgs. 68, 226, 229, 231.
Zamora, Bernice, pgs. 72, 231.

OHIO UNIVERSITY LIBRARY
Please return this book as soon as you have finished with it. In order to avoid a fine it must be returned by the latest date stamped below. All books are subject to recall after two

Printed in the United States
94786LV00002B/198/A